W9-BRQ-859

Red Tape and Housing Costs

Red Tape and Housing Costs

*How Regulation Affects
New Residential Development*

MICHAEL I. LUGER

and

KENNETH TEMKIN

CENTER FOR URBAN POLICY RESEARCH
Edward J. Bloustein School of Planning and Public Policy
Rutgers, The State University of New Jersey
New Brunswick, New Jersey

Published by the CENTER FOR URBAN POLICY RESEARCH
Edward J. Bloustein School of Planning and Public Policy
Civic Square • 33 Livingston Avenue • Suite 400
New Brunswick, New Jersey 08901–1982

Printed in the United States of America

Library of Congress Cataloging-in-Publication Data

Luger, Michael I. (Michael Ian)
    Red tape and housing costs : how regulation affects new residential development /
Michael I. Luger and Kenneth Temkin.
        p.   cm.
    Includes bibliographical references and index.

    ISBN 0-88285-168-3 (alk. paper)

    1. Housing—Law and legislation—Compliance costs—United States. 2. Housing
development—New Jersey—Costs. 3. Bureaucracy. I. Temkin, Kenneth M. II. Title.
KF5730.L84   2000
333.33'822'0973—dc21   00–034042
                                                                    CIP

Cover design: Helene Berinsky

Interior design/typesetting: Arlene Pashman

To Charles Luger

who passed away during the research for this book

☙

County Commissioner, state legislator,
community leader, social service visionary,
he inspired his family, friends, and constituents
to expect the very best from government

He would have endorsed the book's major conclusion:

*There are good regulations that help protect the health,
safety, and welfare of the public
and bad regulations that are wasteful and unnecessary*

Contents

Figures

Tables

Foreword

E veryone knows about red tape. And common sense tells us that government regulation affects the cost of a new house. Indeed, a prominent federal advisory commission reported in 1991 that too many American families cannot find a house they can afford because

> [t]he cost of housing is being driven up by an increasingly expensive and time-consuming permit-approval process, by exclusionary zoning, and by well-intentioned laws aimed at protecting the environment and other features of modern-day life. (U.S. Department of Housing and Urban Development 1991)

But what exactly is the cost of regulation in new housing development? And who pays these costs? Is it the homebuyer, or is it the builder or land developer, or even the seller of the raw land? And if some of the regulation is excessive, how can the housing development regulatory system be reformed?

In the mid-1990s, the New Jersey Department of Community Affairs posed these important public policy question to Housing New Jersey, Inc., a nonprofit organization dedicated to promoting the production and maintenance of sound, secure housing in safe community environments at affordable prices for New Jersey families and individuals. This book provides the answers, based on extensive, multifaceted research in New Jersey and North Carolina. Funded by the State of New Jersey, the study was undertaken by a team led by Professor Michael I. Luger of the Center for Urban and Regional Studies at the University of North Carolina at Chapel Hill.

While scholars in previous decades examined the relationship of government regulations and housing costs (Seidel 1978; Lowry and Ferguson 1992), this is the first book to both quantify the actual, detailed costs of excessive regulation and examine the incidence of regulation—that is, who pays? The distribution of these costs is critical to housing affordability as price increases push new housing beyond the price range of more and more households. At the same time, developers shift to building housing for consumers to whom they can readily pass on the increasing costs of regulation.

State and local governments across America have the power to cut through the housing development red tape and make housing more affordable to more households, but do they have the political will? New Jersey has a growing tradition of housing development policy innovation fueled by pragmatic research, particularly the statewide, mandatory Residential Site Improvement Standards adopted in 1997 and the Rehabilitation Subcode adopted in 1998. Yet the study behind this book was never proudly released. Leaked to New Jersey's largest daily newspaper, its essential finding was headlined on a slow news day's front page: "Excessive permit fees put homes out of reach; Jersey builders face layers of regulation" (*Star-Ledger* 1999).

The unprecedented national economic expansion of the late 1990s and the beginning of the twenty-first century mask for many the deeply entrenched, costly, underlying regulatory morass that governs how and where new housing is built. Luger and Temkin have provided policymakers and housing advocates with hard facts and reasoned explanations about the link between excessive regulations and spiraling housing costs. This information forms the springboard from which policymakers can launch efforts to untangle some of this red tape and create responsible housing development regulatory systems.

DAVID N. KINSEY
Kinsey & Hand, Princeton, New Jersey
Visiting Lecturer in Public and International Affairs
Princeton University

Acknowledgments

We received research assistance and collegial advice from many students and faculty members at the University of North Carolina at Chapel Hill (UNC). Professors Edward J. Kaiser and David R. Godschalk, widely regarded as among the nation's leading experts on land-use planning, helped us design the study in the early stages. Professor William M. Rohe, director of the Center for Urban and Regional Studies at UNC, enabled us to use the good offices of his center as a home base. Spence Cowan, a doctoral student in the Department of City and Regional Planning and a licensed attorney, drafted chapter 3 and helped us understand legal issues. Rob Padgett, a master's degree student in the same department, performed general research assistance.

We also received assistance in New Jersey. Professor David Listokin, codirector of the Center for Urban Policy Research within the Edward J. Bloustein School of Planning and Public Policy at Rutgers, The State University of New Jersey, took a keen interest in this work and helped keep us honest. Kristopher M. Rengert, then a doctoral candidate at the Bloustein School, performed research duties on-site in New Jersey. Dr. Art Wells, formerly at the Wharton School of the University of Pennsylvania and more recently a New Jersey developer, provided invaluable assistance as the New Jersey project manager.

We must also thank the Housing New Jersey Advisory Committee for its oversight and advice during this project. David Kinsey was particularly helpful as a facilitator, critic, and resource. Of the Board members, Amy Fenwick Frank and Michael Gross provided the most extensive comments on our earlier drafts. John Lago, William Connolly, and Cynthia Wilk of the New Jersey Department of Community Affairs (NJDCA) provided excellent comments on the final draft. The New Jersey Home Builders Association and the North Carolina Home Builders Association provided help on the survey. Local planners and engineers in both states provided their time and insights.

Financing for this project was provided by the New Jersey Department of Community Affairs through Housing New Jersey, Inc. Policy statements should be attributed to the authors, not to NJDCA. The authors also assume responsibility for errors of fact or interpretation.

1

Motivation and Conceptual Framework

The American homeownership rate is at an historic high. Since 1992, the overall rate of homeownership has increased from 64.5 percent to a 1999 level of 66.7 percent. In response to this increase in demand for owner-occupied housing, home builders in the last quarter of 1998 alone started 1.3 million new single-family homes. Given these favorable trends, it may seem strange to devote an entire book to the regulatory barriers faced by housing developers. We would agree with that if the robust housing market that started in the early 1990s produced benefits for *all* American families. However, homeownership rates for low- and moderate-income and minority families continue to lag national averages. In 1998, for example, only 46.6 percent of African-American families and 47.0 percent of Hispanic families owned homes, compared to 72.6 percent of white families. Home-ownership rates are also lower for low- and moderate-income families. In addition, homeownership rates have not risen in all states and metropolitan areas. In New Jersey, for example, the rate has barely changed in decades. Indeed, it dropped one-tenth of a percentage point between 1992 and 1999 (from 64.6 to 64.5 percent) (U.S. Bureau of the Census 1999, table 13).

There is no single reason for these discrepancies. In some cases, lower-income families, typically with smaller mortgages, do not benefit from the favorable tax status of the mortgage-interest deduction. For these families,

1

renting may be more desirable than owning a home. In addition, families who expect to move frequently may prefer to rent rather than to pay higher transaction costs associated with selling a home.

Some differences in homeownership rates, then, result from perfectly rational decisions of low- and moderate-income and minority families. Unfortunately, these reasons do not fully account for the differences. More than thirty years after the 1968 Civil Rights Act, which prohibits discrimination by lenders, real estate agents, and other housing market participants, many minority home buyers continue to face discrimination in all aspects of the home-purchase process—beginning with the house-search phase, through prequalification and mortgage underwriting. This discrimination has been demonstrated in studies that use a variety of techniques, including paired-testing and sophisticated econometric analysis of mortgage-origination outcomes.

The relatively low rate of homeownership for low- and moderate-income and minority families and in some states has another likely cause: the prohibitively high prices of homes available for purchase. Indeed, the median price of a newly constructed home in the United States in 1998 was $150,400, whereas the median price nationwide for existing homes sold in 1998 was $131,000.

This "affordability gap" has been addressed by mortgage market institutions, including federal, state, and local governments; Fannie Mae and Freddie Mac; and mortgage originators, including depository lenders, mortgage companies, and savings and loans, by making it easier for low- and moderate-income home buyers to qualify for home mortgages. In most cases, these "affordable lending" or "community lending" initiatives result in mortgage products that allow borrowers to qualify for home purchase loans despite a less-than-perfect credit history, insufficient funds for a down payment, and high total house price (or total debt payment)-to-payment ratio. Some of these programs have been developed in response to the Community Reinvestment Act, which requires lenders to serve all members of communities providing deposits. Other lending programs have been developed in response to regulatory requirements placed on Fannie Mae and Freddie Mac to increase their service to low- and moderate-income families.

These programs are based on the premise that there is a sufficient supply of homes available for purchase by low- and moderate-income families, and that lower-income and minority homeownership rates will increase commensurately with the number of mortgage products tailored to the specific needs of nontraditional borrowers. This assumption is not correct.

Even with more creative mortgage products that allow lower down payments and higher debt-to-income ratios, many low-income and minority families will simply be unable to find homes that are affordable. Government regulations that add unnecessary costs to newly constructed housing reduce the aggregate supply of homes available for all purchasers and particularly affect the ability of low- and moderate-income and minority families to become homeowners. Even modest cost increases disqualify large numbers of families from becoming homeowners.

For us, the question is not simply whether regulation adds to the cost of development. We accept that there are legitimate reasons to limit the type or density of development in an environmentally sensitive place, or to assure that infrastructure capacity is adequate. The key policy question for us is whether there is "excessive" or avoidable regulation that can be reduced or modified without compromising health, safety, and environmental quality.

We also are concerned with the distribution, or incidence, of the costs that are created by regulatory requirements. Builders and developers generally claim that because they must maintain their own bottom lines they pass the costs of regulation on to consumers, which, of course, makes housing less affordable. Yet there could be short-run or anomalous situations in which developers bear some of the regulatory costs in lower rates of return (profits). And developers could also pass regulatory costs backward to land owners by offering less than they would otherwise. That careful distinction among possible incidence paths has not been fully explored in the literature.

This chapter has three parts. First, we define what we mean by "regulation" and its costs. Next, our conceptual framework, which is built on the decision calculus of the developer, is presented. The chapter concludes with a discussion of the importance of the cost and incidence issues.

DEFINING "REGULATION" AND ITS "COSTS"

Regulation is defined here as a variety of required approvals and accompanying payments before, during, and at the completion of the development and building processes. Seidel (1978) identified seven types of government regulations affecting the housing market. Frieden (1983), in turn, identified seven different types of growth restrictions alone. We can distill the large number of regulations into the following three categories:

1. *Zoning and subdivision regulations* that govern the type of activities and capital improvements that can be placed on particular parcels and that specify the standards to which those activities and construction must conform. Zoning, subdivision, and similar applications typically must be accompanied by a fee to offset the cost of review and, in some cases, to provide a financial guarantee of compliance.

2. *Environmental regulations* that are intended to minimize the effect of development on land and waterways, especially in wetlands, coastal zones, near streams, and in other "critical" environmental areas. Those also may be subject to an application fee.

3. *Financial impact regulations,* which include impact fees, hookup charges, and negotiated contributions that are costs of entry and that offset the cost of services that a municipality will be required to provide to new residents.

There are also building regulations (i.e., building codes, most notably the New Jersey Uniform Construction Code). Because they generally tend to vary less from jurisdiction to jurisdiction than do the types of regulation discussed in this book, building codes are not included.[1]

The regulatory language, as codified in ordinances, other legislation, and/or legal interpretations, varies among jurisdictions. For example, variations among New Jersey's municipalities in subdivision requirements led to the promulgation of Uniform Residential Site Improvement Standards in 1996. Many states prepare model zoning ordinances for their municipalities, but they are not always adopted. And states tend to differ in their overall land-use traditions. As a general rule, there is little variation among municipalities in the language of the building codes they apply or in the environmental standards they impose on developers. States and their subdivisions generally subscribe either to BOCA (Building Officials and Code Administrators) or CABO (Council of American Building Officials) building standards, and federal law governs environmental protection.

Even if regulatory language were standard and relatively uniform among jurisdictions, there could be variation in their enforcement and implementation. Burby and May (1996) illustrate that for building codes. The same applies to the other types of regulation.

Regulation is defined here as having several discrete cost elements that can be grouped into five categories:

1. First, there are costs associated with a certain density and intensity of land use stipulated in municipal zoning ordinances. We can call those the *opportunity costs of restricted land use*. For example, if a certain parcel is zoned for six single-family units per acre and environmental review reduces the allowable intensity to two units per acre, there may be a loss in income associated with the regulation.

2. Second, there are *hard costs* associated with the bricks and mortar necessary to meet requirements. For example, to comply with an erosion and sedimentation control ordinance, a developer may have to build retention structures; or a particular subdivision ordinance may require a certain expensive material to be used for curbs.

3. Third, there are *soft costs*, including outlays for the legal, planning, architecture, engineering and environmental consulting, title searches, and surveying required to develop an application. We are particularly interested in the soft costs necessary to meet standards that exceed what the market would have dictated.

4. Fourth, related to those soft costs are *out-of-pocket fees* that must accompany applications.

5. Finally, there are *opportunity costs from delays*: significant costs associated with time delays that a regulatory approval process creates. For example, if an approval is supposed to take 90 days and it actually takes 180 days, there may be lost revenues associated with the delay, increased costs of financing, and possibly costs from "missing the market." Income could be lost for more than just three months in this example if the delay holds up foundation work due to winter weather.

This taxonomy of costs raises a fundamental issue that must be dealt with in all studies on the cost of regulation, that is, what is the "norm" against which costs are calculated? At one extreme, we could specify a hypothetical, fully laissez-faire world as our baseline. Then we would calculate the maximum potential revenue to a developer as determined by market demand (highest and best use) for the product, as well as the physical limitations on meeting that market demand. For example, a parcel in a given location might be most profitable if developed as town homes at 12 units to the acre. The time to completion for those units would be determined by the availability of labor and materials, the logistics of scheduling subcontractors, and the weather. In that case, any zoning that reduces the density and intensity of use at that location, any subdivision requirements that are more costly than what the developer would have provided to meet his or her projection of market demand, and any delays due to regulatory approvals would constitute costs of regulation (i.e., a reduction in the developer's maximum potential revenue).

There are several problems with that approach. First, the counterfactual is always difficult to ascertain. Almost every municipality in the United States has had a system of land-use regulations in place for many decades. Since we do not live in a laissez-faire world, it is difficult to determine what a developer might have surmised as the highest and best use of a parcel. Efficient zoning should reflect market demand to some extent, so we might say that the basic zoning ordinance provides a reasonable proxy for highest and best use. Similarly, there is no accurate way to gauge what consumers would have demanded in terms of landscaping, street widths, sidewalks, curbing materials, and other elements of a subdivision plan. Alternatively, we can regard a subdivision plan as a reasonable representation of community norms.

That notion of community norms is key in determining a baseline. Every community has developed, within a democratic process, an overarching set of principles that relates to health and safety and certain land-use and environmental regulations. Developers are regulated to ensure their compliance with those requirements. For example, it may be more expensive for a developer to provide a buffer between residential property and a busy street, or to provide appropriate access (e.g., complying with sight lines) than not to do so, but such requirements have generally agreed-upon safety purposes. Likewise, building codes often may impose additional costs on developers but are important to achieving the high level of safety society demands. Similarly, erosion and sedimentation requirements and other environmental regulations have a generally agreed-upon intent.

One might argue that consumers would demand development to be done in a safe and healthy manner. However, that is one area in which there is a distinct information asymmetry. Consumers simply are not fully aware of the health and safety properties of materials and site designs or the full costs of environmental damage. As a consequence, builders and developers arguably could build lower-quality projects to meet a similar market demand.

Community norms, on the other hand, can be taken too far as a baseline. As we show in the case studies in chapter 6, community norms differ markedly from place to place. High-income communities that oppose further growth tend to set more rigorous subdivision standards in the name of

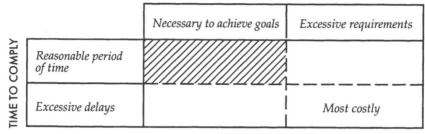

SUBSTANTIVE REGULATIONS

	Necessary to achieve goals	*Excessive requirements*
Reasonable period of time		
Excessive delays		*Most costly*

(with the left axis labeled **TIME TO COMPLY**)

FIGURE 1
Matrix of costs

health and safety than do development-hungry communities. Communities also differ in their willingness to invest in water and sewer and other infrastructure that would allow denser development.

Figure 1 summarizes the discussion of different types of regulation costs. The cells in the matrix represent the following:

- Outlays on regulations that might be considered "reasonable" or "necessary" in order to achieve commonly agreed-upon goals, such as the preservation of health, safety, and environmental quality (column 1)

- Outlays on "excessive" regulations that require developers to incur more hard costs than they would in some baseline case (column 2)

- Costs incurred to comply with regulations in a "reasonable" period of time (row 1)

- Costs incurred due to unnecessary delays (row 2)

To the extent possible, we want to rule out consideration of the upper left cell and ask only about the cases where there are excessive or unnecessary requirements or delays. The most costly regulatory scenario is shown in the lower right cell. Construction of norms or baselines for "reasonable" and "necessary" are discussed below.

A CONCEPTUAL FRAMEWORK

In this study, we walk a fine line between the two views of regulatory costs referred to above: (1) costs incurred to meet government regulations on land use and development, and (2) only those costs that are "excessive" or "unnecessary." We define a baseline in different ways for different types of costs, as reflected in the survey questions we ask. Our general approach is to model a developer's decision calculus. Did he or she know beforehand what the restrictions were and factor them into project planning? How did he or she respond to the restrictions—by seeking to change them? by offering less for the land than he or she otherwise would? by changing project design? by changing the pricing of units? Did he or she miscalculate the costs or delays, or was the builder surprised enough that the bottom line was reduced?

We collected data from North Carolina to provide another benchmark for New Jersey. The choice of North Carolina as the comparison state was driven in part by convenience since the research team was familiar with development and regulatory practices in that state. Our experience in North Carolina led to the judgment that, for several reasons, its regulatory environment is less stringent than that of New Jersey. North Carolina is less densely developed, contains fewer interior wetlands, and has a smaller number of heavily polluting industries.

The decision model that underlies our analysis is characterized in figure 2. The development environment that exists when a developer contemplates a project includes market demand (the types of units the buying public wants built, which is affected by macroeconomic conditions, demographics, and taste), the financial resources available to the developer (which is affected by macroeconomic conditions and the developer's past success), and the regulatory milieu, which includes applicable ordinances and statutes, precedent, and practice in particular places.

Once a developer decides to embark on a project, taking into account the three factors just discussed, he or she attempts to find land that is "priced right." That may mean that it is part of a bankruptcy or under real estate investment trust (REIT) control, so that it is priced under its market value but large enough in size to be affordable only to well-capitalized buyers. Or it may mean a seller will accede to terms the developer considers to be favorable, including a discounted sale price or a sale conditional on obtaining necessary approvals.

The price of land should reflect whether it has approvals in place. If it does, building can begin prior to final approvals for foundations, hookups, or other such items. There may be delays, but they typically will be shorter than in the absence of prior approvals. When land is bought without approvals, the developer must seek them. Whether or not a developer

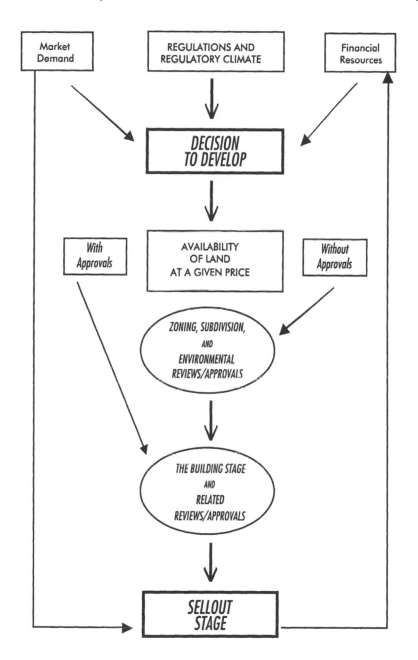

FIGURE 2
A developer's decision calculus

paid a "proper price" for land depends on how long and costly the approval process was relative to what he or she expected.

Naturally, a developer wants to get to the sellout stage as quickly as possible. If there are unexpected delays along the way, market demand may change, making the product difficult to sell at the desired price. If land is bought outright, there are also carrying costs associated with delays.

THE EXTENT AND INCIDENCE
OF REGULATORY COSTS

The timing of the development process and the accuracy of all actors' expectations determine the incidence of the regulatory burden. In a world of perfect information, no surprises, and complete mobility of capital, stricter requirements on developers and longer time delays would not negatively affect developers in the long run. If they acted rationally, they would not stay in the development business if they could not earn a risk-adjusted, economywide, average rate of return. Rather than tie up their resources in building and earn, say, a 6 percent rate of return, they would invest in equities or would manufacture widgets. That would reduce the supply of housing being built and raise the price because of excess demand. More builders would then be induced into the regulated market. The likely long-run incidence, then, is either on homebuyers, who pay higher prices, or landowners, who receive lower offers, or both.

The incidence of the costs of regulation is affected, however, by the fact that there is a limit on what homebuyers can spend annually for a house, typically about 30 percent of gross income. As the cost of regulation drives up housing prices, demand falls and the bottom end of the housing market drops out, leaving mostly high-end houses in the building pipeline. Thus, lower- and middle-income households bear the burden, not simply through higher homeownership costs but because of the lack of homes in their price range. Presumably rents rise as well, in which case there is a loss of consumer surplus. Or there could be a welfare loss due to doubling up, living with parents, living farther away from work where housing is less expensive, and so on.

This burden can be demonstrated for a house that would have sold for $175,000. Assuming an 80 percent, thirty-year conventional mortgage at 8 percent, and using actual tax and insurance data from New Jersey, the homebuyer's PITI (principal, interest, tax, and insurance) payment would be approximately $1,377 per month, requiring a yearly income of $55,000

TABLE 1

Housing Starts in New Jersey

Decade	*Average Starts per Year*
1960s	50,095
1970s	40,561
1980s	37,828
1990s	25,318

Source: New Jersey Department of Labor, Authorized Housing Building
Permit data for indicated years

to qualify. (In addition, of course, a buyer must have the required down
payment and closing costs.) If delays and what is defined here as "excessive" regulation added just $10,000 to the cost of that house, the buyer
would need an income of $57,500 to qualify. According to the 1990 Census,
there are approximately 63,500 New Jersey households with incomes between $55,000 and $57,500. Of course, approximately 70 percent of those
households are already homeowners, but the remainder—almost 20,000
households—are renters who no longer would qualify to buy.

That theorized elimination of housing demand at the lower end of the
market, due to escalating costs, is consistent with data from New Jersey on
housing starts, as shown in table 1.

The 1990s data actually look better now than when the research on this
book project began; during the last three years of the decade, housing starts
averaged 30,507. Up through 1998, the 1990s average was barely 25,000!

Of course, the decline in starts illustrated above likely was caused by
many factors, including demographic shifts. But many also believe that
New Jersey builders and developers have been subjected to a particularly
costly amount of regulation. The New Jersey Builders Association states,
for example, that:

> It is clear to any who look at the data that New Jersey's economic distress
> is the result of regional (i.e., state-specific)—not national—factors. It re-
> flects the combined effects of ill-advised policies and overbearing regu-
> lations that discourage enterprise, diminish competitiveness and, ulti-
> mately, strangle economic growth. (New Jersey Builders Association 1995)

Increases in housing prices and a slowdown of starts together would seem to account for a reduction in homeownership rates in the United States. That rate fell nationally during the 1980s from 65.6 percent to 64.1 percent. Though modest, the decrease masks a large decrease in the number of young families who own homes. In 1973, for example, 51.4 percent of households with a head between 25 and 34 years of age owned their homes. By 1990, only 44.3 percent of such families were homeowners (Stegman et al. 1995). For many young families, the down payment required by lenders to qualify for a mortgage and the carrying costs of a home represent insurmountable hurdles to homeownership.

Whether the decline in demand for housing at the lower- and middle-income end of the market, as just described, is a direct consequence of regulation as opposed to being simply contemporaneous is an empirical question that has been addressed in the literature. Unfortunately, that literature provides policymakers with a welter of conflicting and inconclusive information regarding the impact of regulations on the housing market.

This book answers policymakers' need for detailed information about the impact of specific regulations on the process of delivering newly constructed homes to market. There is yet a broader question regarding the efficiency of regulations in general. Thus, the book examines another question: Can government regulation in the housing market be justified by its social benefits beyond the costs borne by landowners, builders, or homebuyers?

Chapter 2 reviews issues associated with previous studies about the effects of regulation on housing prices. It describes the methodological challenges associated with conducting such studies and points out the complexities involved in interpreting their results. Chapter 3 addresses what we consider the most important aspect of the problem—the procedural delays that add to developers' costs. Chapter 4 uses survey results from regulators and developers/builders in New Jersey and North Carolina to assess the difference between regulatory intent and actual outcomes. Chapter 5 presents different types of evidence about the monetary costs of regulation: from the surveys of developers/builders and from an econometric model that analyzes the relationship between a municipality's regulatory restrictiveness and housing starts. Chapter 6 presents information from in-depth case studies conducted in New Jersey and North Carolina about how developers and government officials perceive the effects of government regulations in specific municipal contexts. Chapter 7 summarizes the key findings and discusses their implications for policy. The report also includes two appendices. Appendix I contains material about environmental regulation in North Carolina; Appendix II elaborates on the research design and methodological issues.

2

Previous Studies About Regulation and Housing Costs

overnment restrictions on the use of private land date back to the early 1900s. Beginning with housing reformers such as Jane Addams and Jacob Riis, early regulations were designed to ensure that newly built housing was constructed in a manner consistent with a healthy physical environment.

Land-use restrictions came next, intended initially to segregate economic activities with potentially harmful side effects from residential communities (Levy 1994). Shortly thereafter, single- and multifamily dwellings were also separated, a practice upheld by the Supreme Court in 1926 in *Village of Euclid v. Ambler Realty Co.*[2] With the constitutionality of zoning established, states were free, within the limits of the police power and takings clause, to control land uses in any given location. Regulations governing subdivision of land evolved from minimal plat requirements to more extensive review of layout and infrastructure during the same period. Control over land use and subdivision became the exclusive province of municipalities as states delegated their power to local governments in the belief that impacts from development were primarily local (Briffault 1990). That pattern was the dominant model until the early 1970s.

The increase in the number of governmental authorities issuing regulations has made the process more complex. Local government is no longer the sole permitting body for residential development. Frequently, developers must meet requirements set by several authorities, and those requirements are not always consistent. Sometimes a regional or state agency sets performance standards to be enforced by local officials; in other cases, an agency issues permits and imposes conditions itself.

IS REGULATION ALWAYS BAD?

In order for an economic market to be efficient, the price faced by buyers and sellers should reflect all of the costs associated with a particular commodity. Prices of commodities frequently do not include all costs associated with their use. For example, the price of steel includes the costs of raw materials needed for its production and workers employed by the steel company, as well as the costs of shipping the final product to its ultimate destination. However, the costs associated with pollution resulting from the production process are not included in the final sales price of steel. Such side effects, called externalities, impose social costs in the form of increased pollution-related illnesses and environmental degradation (Mueller 1989). In order for government regulation to be efficient, the price paid by consumers for a product must be increased to equal the costs associated with production as well as the expenses to society created by externalities.

This is the core of the problem. It is very difficult to calculate the social costs of various uses of land. Even if it were possible, given the complex interactions between land use and social costs, it is highly unlikely that government restrictions could be calibrated in such a way that increased costs to landowners or housing consumers would equal the increased cost to society resulting from more intensive land use. Consequently, land-use restrictions have a very high probability of inefficiency—that is, the costs generated by government regulations exceed the social costs derived from changing land-use patterns.

REGULATION AND HOMEOWNERSHIP RATES

A second basis for opposing government restrictions on land use is related to the aforementioned cost factor but is more specific in its focus. Unnecessary regulations, according to detractors, can increase the costs of housing beyond the reach of many low- and moderate-income Americans. Some critics attribute the declining rates of homeownership in the 1980s to an increase in the scope and complexity of government regulations. (Given the upswing in overall homeownership rates in the late 1990s, this argument would have to apply to the lower-income and younger segments of the population, who have not enjoyed greater access to homeownership.)

The connection made between regulation and a declining rate of homeownership is, to some degree, a function of timing. Many government regulations on land use and housing construction were implemented in the 1970s in response to growing concern about unchecked property development. At the same time, the after-tax cash cost of owning a home was increasing. In 1988 dollars, the annual after-tax cash cost of homeownership increased from a 1967 rate of $5,801 to $9,672 in 1980 (Apgar 1990, table 2.5). As previously noted, this affected homeownership rates, especially in the 1980s and particularly for young families.

No one disputes that increased government regulation was contemporaneous with declining rates of homeownership. However, the degree to which increased regulation actually *caused* and was not merely correlated with declining homeownership rates has not been established. One would expect that the literature on regulation and housing would provide a clear analysis of the effect of separate regulations on each stage of the home-building process. Yet, a review of that literature does not provide answers that would help to resolve the debate regarding the desirability of government regulations affecting housing (Fischel 1990).

This book is motivated in large part by policymakers' need for detailed information regarding the impact of specific regulations on the process of delivering newly constructed homes to the market. As we will discuss, the extant literature provides policymakers with a welter of conflicting and inconclusive information concerning the impact of regulations on the housing market. We are also cognizant of the broader question regarding the efficiency of regulations in general. Consequently, we seek to address how government regulations affecting the housing market can be justified by their social benefits, despite the attendant costs that must be borne by someone: landowner, builder, or home buyer.

GENERAL ISSUES IN THE LITERATURE ON REGULATION AND HOUSING

For many reasons, determining the effect of regulations on housing prices is difficult. One problem is that there are numerous types of government regulations that affect the production of housing. Seidel (1978) identified no fewer than seven types of government regulations affecting the housing market. Frieden (1983) pointed out seven different types of growth restrictions alone—one of the seven categories discussed by Seidel. The upshot here is that it is difficult enough to isolate the effect from the existing literature of any one classification of restrictions, let alone a more finely defined regulation within a class of restrictions.

Moreover, it is important to bear in mind that housing production consists of many steps, from purchasing raw land to acquiring approval for any zoning reclassification through site plan development and securing permits. All this activity must occur before construction actually begins. Consequently, although there are studies that estimate the dollar impact of regulations on housing production, they often do not examine *how* regulations affect the decisions of housing producers at each stage in the production process.

In general, studies on the effect of government regulation differ with respect to the type of data employed and the ensuing statistical techniques used to reach conclusions. The first set of studies utilizes multiple regression in order to ascertain the effect of government regulation on the sales price of houses. This technique, sometimes called hedonic analysis, assumes that the market value of a house reflects the tax-service/regulation mix in that community, neighborhood amenities, and individual features of the unit itself, including the number of bedrooms and baths, overall volume, quality of materials, and so on. Hedonic estimation statistically disaggregates the contribution of each community, neighborhood, and house-specific attribute to the market price of the asset (Rothenberg et al. 1991). A hedonic analysis, for example, may indicate that each "unit" of regulation adds $100 to the value of the house, or an additional bedroom is worth $500. That creates some obvious scaling challenges, such as the appropriate metric for regulation.

The second major category of studies involves either detailed case studies or uses data gathered from surveys or interviews. These approaches usually compare the costs of developing housing in areas with relatively restrictive regulatory environments to costs associated with home construction in jurisdictions with less-burdensome regulations. The advantage to these studies is that a more detailed analysis of the costs associated with each type of restriction can be estimated. The literature based on hedonic estimates is discussed first, followed by a review of analyses based on either case studies or survey data.

Hedonic Studies

Empirical studies on the effects of regulations on housing prices date back to the mid-1960s (for an excellent review of these earlier studies, see Mills 1972). The attention paid to this topic increased as more local governments adopted regulations in the mid- to late 1970s in an attempt to slow local development. Studies conducted in the late 1970s through the mid-1980s sought to assess the effects of these regulations. In general, initiatives to slow growth utilized zoning restrictions, so many of these studies focused on zoning's effect on housing market outcomes (see, for example, Dowall and Landis 1982; Goldberg and Horwood 1980; Jud 1980; and Mark and Goldberg 1983, 1986).

These studies did not generate a consensus as to the effect of government regulation on housing. In fact, Mark and Goldberg (1986, 259) indicate that "opinions differ as to the property value impacts of zoning and as to whether negative externalities exist." Pasha (1996) suggests that these divergent findings result from the complexities involved in specifying models and making necessary assumptions in order to create tractable research projects.

Interpretation Issues

Hedonic estimation of the effect of regulation on house prices is subject to issues of interpretation as well as of methodology. An increase in housing prices results from either an upward shift in the marginal cost curve faced by producers of housing (prompted by increased input costs), increased demand for housing by consumers who are willing to pay a higher unit price for housing in an area with growth restrictions, or some combination of these factors (Pogodzinski and Sass 1990). As a result, an increase in housing prices in communities with a greater degree of government regulation may not reflect higher costs of land or delays in securing a project's approval. Rather, it may reflect potential purchasers' belief that growth restrictions will lead to lower population densities, thereby enhancing their desire to own housing in the municipality.

Wachter and Cho (1991) developed nomenclature to distinguish between these two effects. A scarcity effect occurs from increasing costs of inputs resulting from regulation, whereas an amenity effect is a by-product of creating a more attractive residential environment through government intervention. The contributions of these effects to housing price changes are not easy to differentiate.

The effect of government regulations on housing prices also depends on the openness of housing markets and relative land availability. If the region's housing market is "open," greater restrictiveness in one community will drive development to another nearby, less-restrictive location, assuming developable land is available there and that any additional commute time is offset by the additional amenities from larger dwellings and more land (Fujita 1989). Therefore, one jurisdiction's regulations may have a spillover effect, increasing the rate of housing development in nearby communities with fewer regulatory restrictions. In some cases, development may leapfrog entire communities with highly complex regulatory environments, such as when housing production moved from Marin to Sonoma County, California (Frieden 1983).

If a city's housing market can be described as "open," then any increase in housing prices results from the amenity effect, so that lower population densities in more highly regulated jurisdictions closer to the central business district produce higher bids for housing. If developable land is not available (due to buildout or a region's topography, for example) or consumers do not view more distant homes as perfect substitutes, then the city's housing market is closed. Price increases in a closed city result from the scarcity effect, whereby the costs of inputs used to produce housing increase.

Wachter and Cho (1991) found evidence of intrajurisdictional effects (scarcity and amenity) as well as an interjurisdictional effect in a study of new housing prices in Montgomery County, Maryland. Intrajurisdictional effects raised the price of housing while reducing the value of land in a more restrictive municipality. In addition, the price for housing and raw land in communities bordering areas with regulation increased, but this interjurisdictional effect was smaller than the intrajurisdictional effect. Eliott (1981) looked at the average price of single-family homes in fifty cities in California between 1969 and 1976 in order to assess the effect of regulation on housing prices in both open and closed cities. Regulation had a much greater effect in "closed" cities with growth controls (and therefore fewer substitutes) than in other nearby "open" communities that had looser regulatory environments.

The decline in raw land prices in a jurisdiction adopting regulations results from the capitalization of an increase in the developer's costs of producing housing. However, this effect is not so straightforward. Although a developer will face a delay in developing raw land into housing in a jurisdiction with controls, the attractiveness of the neighborhood may be enhanced by the restrictions adopted by the municipal government. Consequently, raw land in areas with restrictions may increase in value so long as the amenity effect offsets cost increases created by delays (Brueckner 1990). Fischel (1990) argues that since land prices represent the expected net present value of future rent, limiting land use to large-lot, single-family homes will reduce land prices because land zoned for higher densities can have more revenue-generating dwelling units. Furthermore, agricultural land legally precluded from future development commands a lower price on the market than unrestricted agricultural land.

Although somewhat confusing, hedonic estimates of the effect of government regulation on housing prices do sometimes indicate that restrictions increase the cost of housing; homes in more restrictive regulatory environments are more expensive than identical units in areas with less government intervention. This conclusion is subject to several caveats, however. First, nearly all studies utilizing hedonic estimates on the effect of government regulation have a methodological error. Schwartz, Zorn, and Hanson (1986, 236) take issue with Dowall and Landis's approach to modeling the housing market in the Bay Area, an approach that stratifies by quality. The problem with using dummy variables for different types of markets is that "It does not estimate separate implicit prices for each community. . . . Not allowing for implicit prices to vary across communities can be a source for bias." Schwartz, Zorn, and Hanson advise researchers to estimate hedonic parameter estimates for each community, ideally by year, in order to assess the impact of government regulations.

Even if they are methodologically sound, hedonic estimates of regulations fail to distinguish between scarcity, amenity, or spillover effects. Consequently, attempts to interpret estimates of government intervention derived from hedonic regressions fail to identify the cause of higher housing prices. Amenity effects, rather than a cost, could be interpreted as a benefit to purchasers who are willing to pay a higher price for more housing in more desirable neighborhoods. Furthermore, as alluded to in the discussion of open versus closed cities, the availability of substitutes in a housing market further complicates the use of hedonic regression. This is a particular point within a more general issue. Hedonic estimates use the price of housing as the dependent variable. However, the price changes do not represent the increased costs faced by housing producers as the result of government regulations. The elasticity of demand for housing in a municipality affects the degree to which housing producers can pass along cost increases to purchasers. Consequently, other studies of government regulation have relied less on hedonic estimates of housing prices and more on case studies and surveys of developers actually involved in the production of housing. This approach allows a more detailed focus on how different regulations affect different areas of housing production. In addition, obtaining information from developers provides information about costs borne by the supplier as well as those passed along to the consumer. Securing primary data is, unfortunately, a necessary evil if one is to conduct a detailed analysis of costs in the housing industry. Lowry and Ferguson (1992, 8) lamented how their "fieldwork disabused us of some ideas about the availability of systematic data on land use and development activity in American cities."

Case Studies and Survey Analyses

One of the most comprehensive studies of regulation and housing costs, utilizing surveys and interviews, was done by Seidel (1978). His results were based on 300 interviews with key informants involved in developing and monitoring local regulations pertaining to housing construction, as well as information provided in 2,500 questionnaires returned from a mailing to 33,000 home builders. Seidel's book quantifies the effect of seven types of government regulations on housing construction costs and, in doing so, provides one of the most detailed pictures of how each stage in the construction process is affected by government regulations. His approach is consistent with the research methodology advocated by Johnston, Schwartz, and Hunt (1984, 8), who argue that "[i]n order to understand the effect of government regulations, one should first look at the cost to the builder of each regulation."

Building Codes

Mandated building codes are the first type of regulatory requirement discussed by Seidel. Municipalities often adopt/adapt model building codes promulgated by the construction industry for the states. Seidel argues that building codes frequently have little technical justification and require building technology that is out of date. For example, ABS pipe, invented in 1948, was not incorporated in a model building code until 1966; it was later still that it was adopted by localities in their own building codes. Home builders frequently are hampered in their efforts to adopt new technologies that may reduce construction costs. A Colorado study (White 1992) that analyzed the effect of building codes between 1970 and 1975 found that safety requirements increased the price of the average new house by $1,100, or 5 percent.

Subdivision Requirements

Subdivision requirements have also grown more complex, and in the eyes of developers, much more onerous. Originally, subdivision requirements outlined the relatively simple steps necessary to transform raw land (a plat) into parcels suitable for development, such as mapping tracts and generating title and deeds for the plots within the subdivision. More recently, subdivision requirements have begun to include stipulations about infrastructure that must be provided by the developer, width of streets, and so on. These improvement standards, according to Seidel, represent nothing more than "gold-plating." Such standards require developers to provide amenities that are unnecessary and, in doing so, preclude the construction of more affordable housing in suburban communities with costly subdivision requirements. There are others who do not agree, however. White (1992), in case studies of Boulder, Colorado, and Ramapo, New York, found that a relatively strict regulatory environment was not incompatible with the construction of housing affordable to low- and moderate-income families.

Zoning and Growth Management Restrictions

Building codes and subdivision requirements relate directly to construction costs. The next two types of costs analyzed by Seidel are the result of zoning and growth management techniques, which restrict the types of housing that can be built in a community. The effect is more indirect but of equal importance to the developer. Unfortunately, assessing the impact of zoning and growth controls utilizing survey data is as difficult as measuring the effect with hedonic analysis. According to Seidel (1978, 176–77), "[t]he impact of zoning restrictions on the price of raw land is the most elusive aspect of zoning's cost effects due to the wide variation in real estate market conditions."

Lowry and Ferguson (1992) were less ambiguous in their findings. The authors looked at the effect of government regulations in three growing metropolitan areas—Sacramento, California; Nashville, Tennessee; and

Orlando, Florida—in order to assess the effect of restrictions on housing prices. Sacramento, either through zoning or limiting infrastructure, had only 40,000 acres available for residential construction, compared to 90,000 acres in Nashville and 100,000 acres in Orlando. Although all three cities experienced strong increases in demand for housing during the 1980s, Sacramento, with the most restrictive regulatory environment, had the highest rate of increase in housing prices.

Rosen and Katz (1981, 339) also looked at regulations' effects on housing prices by analyzing their impact on the development of 700 single-family homes on a 300-acre site in a medium-sized jurisdiction on the fringes of the Bay Area. Housing developers in this region must pay impact fees, one-time fixed charges that represent the marginal costs to the town's budget for providing infrastructure to the subdivision. Impact fees became an important source of revenue in California after Proposition 13 limited local governments' ability to increase revenue through higher property taxes (Rosen and Katz 1981, 329). According to their analysis, fees totaled $7,140, with a $1,785 city sewer connection as the largest component.

RESPONDING TO REGULATIONS

Rosen and Katz's case study also highlights how developers must adopt strategies to cope with a complex regulatory environment by not building in areas with restrictive regulations or by proposing subdivisions that exceed even the most restrictive subdivision regulations. Following the second strategy usually entails hiring staff to negotiate with municipalities and doing what needs to be done to assure development approval (Rosen and Katz 1981, 338). Both the organizational costs created by restrictions and the permit fees increased the price of newly constructed homes in this city from $75,000 to $90,000. Because there was a strong demand for housing in the area, those cost increases were ultimately paid for by the purchaser.

Although building codes, subdivision requirements, and impact fees all increase the costs of housing by requiring developers to include amenities that they otherwise might not provide, there is another effect that is even more important. By making the development process more complex, the time it takes to convert raw land to housing is lengthened. In addition, as alluded to by Rosen and Katz, the number of permits and official approvals that must be secured increases the probability of delay. In Sacramento, for example, Lowry and Ferguson estimated that the costs of delay added $26,000, or about 20 percent, to the price of a newly constructed house. Seidel (1978) estimated that every one-month delay in the time needed to complete a project increases the cost of housing by 1.2 percent.

Johnston, Schwartz, and Hunt (1984) provide one of the most detailed pictures of how delay makes housing development more costly. They show that in Davis, California, the development of a typical twenty-five-unit subdivision would cost $1.4 million. Of that, $130,000 would be spent in the preliminary approval stage, covering any rezonings and acquisitions of subdivision maps. Sometimes the developer subcontracts this activity to a "paper subdivider" who makes no improvements on raw land but secures permits needed by a developer to begin land conversion (Lowry and Ferguson 1992, 96-97). Delays during this process increase the costs to the developer by $3,692 per month. The next stage involves site improvements (preparing raw land for home construction), such as clearing land, constructing sewers, and building sidewalks. That stage is more complex, costing the developer $220,000. Because more capital has been invested by the developer by the time the second stage ends, monthly costs of delay during this period increase to $5,067. Finally, construction costs for this twenty-five-unit subdivision are $1.05 million. Delays during this period are very costly, rising to $13,004 per month.

Nichols et al. (1982) also emphasize the potential impact of delays on housing costs and the importance of the interest rate. Nichols (1981) points out how stretching the lead time required for a developer to construct housing increases the time a housing market will be out of equilibrium. Longer lead times increase the probability that a developer will "miss-time" the market and/or reduce his or her ability to respond to rapid changes in an area's housing market.

These case studies provide a more detailed description of the impact of government regulations on housing prices. Rather than relying on published house price data, they used information elicited directly from housing producers. Nichols (1981) combined secondary and primary data collection approaches in a study of the impact of Florida's adoption of the American Law Institute's Model Land Development Code on areas of critical environmental concern. Developers provided cost figures for nine projects that were subject to the provisions of the new code. On average, the regulations increased per-unit construction costs by $550, with land dedications making up the largest component. In addition, Nichols conducted a hedonic regression of home prices across regulated and unregulated areas using a dummy variable to measure the effect of regulation.

The parameter estimate for the dummy variable was $4,700; it was significant only at the 0.10 level of confidence. Given this discrepancy, Nichols argued that the true cost of regulation in Florida is the higher number, because the developer may not bear all of the costs brought about by distortions in the market that are caused by regulations.

WHO PAYS THE COST OF REGULATION?

Nichols's study, combining the two major research methodologies discussed thus far (hedonics and case studies), highlights the difficulty of assessing the impact of government regulations on the price of housing. Increased costs to developers brought about by government restrictions are not always passed along to consumers. Many hedonic studies of the impacts of growth controls analyzed the California housing market in the 1970s, in part because academics in California saw an opportunity to measure the effects of growth controls in that state in the wake of legislation adopted in the 1970s (Fischel 1990). Generalizing to all other states and markets may be problematic. As Frieden (1983, 134) notes, developers "are able to pass along to consumers most cost impacts of growth restrictions in California because demand is strong and people buy in anticipation of further inflation." In other words, consumers participating in the California housing market in the 1970s may have had relatively inelastic demand curves, thereby affecting the degree to which regulations affected housing prices. In addition, many of the studies mentioned looked more specifically at the Bay Area housing market, which, due to geography (San Francisco is located on an isthmus), more closely represents a closed city, thereby exacerbating the effects of government intervention.

DEREGULATION AND AFFORDABLE HOUSING

As mentioned earlier, there are two major concerns expressed by opponents of government regulation. All of the studies we have reviewed conclude that government regulation does increase the cost of housing. Indeed, because regulations aim to make the price of a house reflect its social costs, prices under regulation should increase. Malpezzi (1994, 1) sardonically writes, "[n]o one would ever be, or should be, surprised at a finding that regulations raise housing prices. That is exactly what they are designed to do." Most of the studies, however, point out that increases in prices exceed the benefits derived from mandated open space requirements, higher-quality building codes, and similar restrictions. Therefore, there is a general consensus that regulation is inefficient in the sense that the increases in construction costs that are attributable to them are greater than the externalities generated from the increase in residential construction.

The second theme—that regulations have affected homeownership rates—does not generate such a consensus. Testifying before a congressional hearing on this very issue, Mandelker (1990, 3) argued that blaming declining rates of homeownership on government regulation "is highly oversimplified. Housing affordability is a complex problem, and land-use constraints are one and not even a major contributor to housing costs." Downs (1991, 1098) strongly disagreed, asserting that government regulations increase housing costs by 50 percent. Fischel (1990, 8) concurred, stating that "growth controls are important contributors [to housing prices], raising the cost of housing by at least 10 percent and maybe as much as 30 to 40 percent."

Has government regulation decreased homeownership rates? The question is open for debate. One point must be kept in mind. Almost all of the studies in the literature analyze the effect of government regulation on house prices in suburban municipalities. In addition, hedonic estimates concentrate on land-use policies, not building codes. The Kean Commission, a HUD-sponsored panel chaired by the former governor of New Jersey, noted the importance of that tilt, since reduced construction activity in cities is due more to building codes than to suburban-type regulations. "These codes often require state-of-the-art materials and methods inconsistent with those originally used." Unfortunately, there are few systematic studies quantifying the effect of building codes on housing prices, although the Kean Commission's report indicates that excessive rehabilitation codes add $4,000 to dwelling costs in cities (U.S. Department of Housing and Urban Development 1991, 6).

Zoning restrictions, growth controls, impact fees, and other such regulations tend to be more prevalent in suburban than in central-city jurisdictions. To the extent that the relaxation of those regulations can exert downward pressure on housing prices (as the empirical literature focusing on suburbs shows), deregulation would reduce housing prices more in the suburbs than in central cities,[3] having the effect of inducing central-city renters to move to the suburbs to purchase the now more affordable housing. However, city renters sometimes confront other barriers when they attempt to purchase homes in suburban communities, for example, racial steering by real estate agents (Farley et al. 1993). As a result, it is difficult to predict how homeownership rates will be affected by reducing land-use regulations. Moreover, since the financial impact of building codes on housing construction is not well known, it is difficult to predict how changes to those codes will affect the rate of new construction in cities, which is where many low- and moderate-income renters live.

In this book we consider the impact of regulations on housing prices in both suburban and central-city jurisdictions as a way to advance our knowledge about the distributional effects of those regulations and the likelihood that regulatory reform will make suburban housing more affordable for low- and moderate-income families.

3

The Regulatory Process in New Jersey and North Carolina

M any stakeholders, particularly developers, are convinced that the
existing regulatory system in New Jersey causes unnecessary expense and delays in the residential development and building process, driving up the cost of the finished product and, arguably, tilting the mix of new housing toward the higher end of the income scale.

To claim that regulation in New Jersey is too expensive and time-consuming does not necessarily imply that development should be unregulated. There is widespread agreement among regulators and developers, owners and buyers, that some degree of regulation is necessary to protect public health, safety, and welfare, and to preserve property values. The complaint is with the excessive costs imposed and the unnecessary delays in granting approvals. The challenge is to reduce the cost of regulatory compliance and delay without diminishing the protections those regulations provide to health, safety, welfare, and environmental quality.

The regulation of residential development and building has substantive and procedural dimensions. Substantive regulation includes, for example, density limits, infrastructure specifications, wetlands protection, and tree preservation requirements. In some instances, those requirements or regulations are no more than what a developer would need to provide to ensure a marketable product or an appropriate measure of protection for the public. However, regulations may set substantive standards that are beyond what is essential or reasonable in order to accomplish the purposes for which they ostensibly were adopted. As stated earlier, the difference in cost between theoretically reasonable substantive requirements and those that are actually imposed is what we define in this study as "excessive."

Procedural delays occur as a natural consequence of the permitting process. Proposals must be reviewed to ensure compliance with applicable ordinances, and that inevitably takes time, which adds to a developer's cost. A review may be technical, ensuring that the plan submitted meets the letter of the regulations. It usually also involves discretionary issues, and the rules may require that a decision-making board hold a public hearing. The time spent reviewing is necessary to accomplish substantive regulatory objectives and to accord all stakeholders due process. However, when the approval process takes more than what should be needed to accomplish those objectives, the delay is "unnecessary."

This chapter focuses on the procedural aspects of development permitting because the added expenses that result from unnecessary delay are costs without benefits. It may be argued that regulations that set unreasonable substantive standards add amenity value to a project, providing some marginal improvement or benefit. Conversely, unnecessary delay does not add to the quality or value of a final product; neither does it further regulatory objectives. This chapter focuses on the development process in New Jersey, with North Carolina used for comparison. The stylized process we describe is derived from the common elements of subdivision and other plan review procedures in municipalities in both states.

The use of North Carolina as a comparison state is not intended to allow generalizations to be drawn from the study. We recognize that there are important differences between the two states that limit their comparability. New Jersey, for example, is the country's most urban state, whereas North Carolina has a high percentage of its population living in nonmetropolitan counties. New Jersey's land is fully divided into incorporated municipalities; North Carolina still has unincorporated areas. Both states have long coastlines, but New Jersey has more inland wetlands. In addition, New Jersey has a long legacy of industrial development, with highly polluting petrochemical facilities.

Some important differences between the two states are reflected in table 2. The median North Carolina household spends a lower share of its income on housing than does the median New Jersey household. In addition, per capita property tax burdens are considerably different. New Jersey

TABLE 2

Differences between New Jersey and North Carolina

Category		New Jersey	North Carolina
Population (estimated)	(1999)	8,178,000	7,777,000
Median household income	(1990)	$41,000	$27,000
Median house value	(1990)	$162,300	$65,800
Ratio, median house value to median household income		4:1	2.5:1
Per capita property tax	(1992)	$1,269	$374
Property tax rank		2	40

Source: U.S. Census Bureau, *Statistical Abstract*, for property tax and median household income data; U.S. Census Bureau, *1990 Census of Population*, for median house value; U.S. Census Bureau, Population Estimates Program, Population Division, Table ST-99-1 for 1999 population estimates. 1990 data are presented for median household income to comport with year of housing value data; income figures for 1995 were $44,342 (New Jersey) and $34,076 (North Carolina).

localities depend more on local property taxes for schools and other local services. The higher relative cost of housing suggests that costly regulations may be at work in New Jersey. The difference in fiscal structure suggests that land-use and zoning decisions are influenced more by the practice of "home rule" in New Jersey municipalities than jurisdictions in North Carolina.

GENERAL PROCEDURAL REQUIREMENTS IN THE REGULATION OF LAND USE

The general approval process—for subdivision or (re)zoning requests—is shown in figure 3. Obviously, the details will differ from state to state. Those differences may explain some of the variations in procedural delays that are observed between New Jersey and North Carolina.

The process begins with the developer submitting the plan to the appropriate office in the municipality. Ideally, he or she will have worked with staff in the municipality while preparing the plan in order to ensure that the material submitted is complete and in compliance with the applicable regulations. Jurisdictions often differ in the amount of detail required at this stage and the amount of interaction necessary prior to formal review.

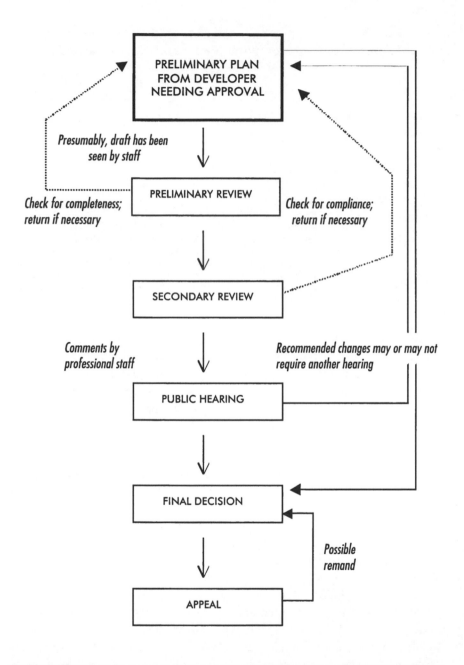

PRELIMINARY PLAN
FROM DEVELOPER
NEEDING APPROVAL

*Presumably, draft has been
seen by staff*

PRELIMINARY REVIEW

*Check for completeness;
return if necessary*

*Check for compliance;
return if necessary*

SECONDARY REVIEW

*Comments by
professional staff*

*Recommended changes may or may not
require another hearing*

PUBLIC HEARING

FINAL DECISION

*Possible
remand*

APPEAL

FIGURE 3
General flow in approval process

When the application is deemed complete, typically it is sent for technical review or impact assessment. If more detail is needed at that stage, the developer may be asked to supplement the submission. The technical compliance review or impact assessment is performed by either heads of departments, staff, or consultants, depending on how a municipality operates. Reviewers must ensure that a project complies with applicable ordinances or determine how a zoning change will affect the community's long-range comprehensive plan. If there are deficiencies, the staff returns the plan to the developer, with comments, or outlines the issues in writing. The developer then makes changes necessary to address the deficiencies and resubmits the plan. The process begins again.

Once the technical review determines that a plan fully or essentially complies with all ordinances, or is consistent with the community's comprehensive plan, the staff forwards it to the decision-making body—for example, a planning board (in New Jersey) or a town or city council (in most North Carolina municipalities). That decision-making body may or may not ask for a recommendation from staff. Final approval requires a public hearing, where further comments from the community are considered. The discussion among the decision makers, and by the public, may lead the body to return the plan to the developer for modification. Or, the body may vote to approve or deny the request as it stands. If modifications are requested, the decision makers may require another public hearing, or they may approve the plan conditionally pending staff review of the required changes.

Some municipalities issue special-use or conditional-use permits for development. Under that system, applications are considered on their merits, as individual cases, rather than in terms of their compliance with a general ordinance. This alternative typically is invoked when land uses are deemed to have special characteristics (large parcels or special mixed use, for example). Those permits still require evidence that the proposed use will have no adverse effect on public health, safety, and welfare, property values, or the comfort and convenience of the public in general. A permit may be issued with reasonable conditions and safeguards attached as preconditions. As a general rule, a proposed use must be of such location, size, and character as to be in harmony with the appropriate and orderly development of the area. The use cannot be detrimental to the orderly development of adjacent properties in accordance with the zone classification of those properties.

Court appeal is the final step in the process, but few development decisions proceed that far. State law determines who has standing, the elements of a prima facie case, and who has the burden of proof as to each element. That is not a matter of local control but an essential element in the approval process. Of all the stages, court appeal is the most protracted and costly to both a developer and a locale, usually consuming more time and money than all other steps of the process.

REGULATION AS THE BALANCING OF STAKEHOLDER INTERESTS

The fundamental elements in the approval process are common to municipalities in both New Jersey and North Carolina: They are designed to protect the interests of all stakeholders, including the general public, neighbors, others whose interests may be more affected than members of the public at large, and the developer. These elements also establish the balance of power among those competing interests. Some municipalities have added a variety of mandatory and optional steps to the basic process, and some states have added procedural stages at either the regional or state level. Among the latter are advisory boards for specific areas or with specific functional jurisdiction, such as site design or wetlands protection. The addition of such supplementary reviews or approvals may alter the balance among the various stakeholders, favoring some over others, depending upon the mandate establishing the extra step(s). Whether an additional step changes the balance or not, it adds to the time and cost of the approval process. That cost may be justified if the same balance could not be attained by substantive requirements administered through the basic process.

Without a reasonable balancing of protection for stakeholder interests, the regulations would appear to sacrifice the interests of one group or individual, which might ultimately be to the detriment of all, since stakeholders may play different roles in different situations. In addition, balance in local procedures is needed in order to preserve the viability of the nonjudicial decision-making function of the system. Without adequate opportunity for all interests to be considered in a local permitting process, those who believe they are excluded may be more likely to resort to judicial intervention as their chosen means of protection.

A technical compliance review protects the general public's interests by assuring that developers are fulfilling the requirements of the governing ordinances that are in force. Only proposals that comply with existing rules are passed by the reviewers. The ordinances should specify the basis upon which a variance or waiver requested by a developer might be allowed. In New Jersey, use variances are provided by the Municipal Land

Use Law. But in both New Jersey and North Carolina, a developer's submission must demonstrate that the request for an exception is within the scope of variances allowable under the ordinance. For example, if a developer requested a use variance because of financial hardship, the reviewers could find that request in compliance only if the ordinance allowed financial hardship as an exception; even so, it might not be granted.

Neighbors are stakeholders whose interests may diverge from the general public good. New development has the potential to change the character of a neighborhood, cause traffic congestion, overburden infrastructure, or lower property values. Those effects are most pronounced in areas immediately adjacent to a development site; they diminish with distance. Thus, neighbors are impacted differently from the general public, making the nature of their interest distinct. Their interests are protected first by the limitations spelled out in the ordinances. In addition, neighbors, through planning board public hearings, have a specific opportunity to influence boards on any discretionary decisions that might be connected to an application. Finally, through the standing rules of the judicial system, neighbors lacking proof of special harm are nonetheless guaranteed access to the courts for the protection of their interests.

Other affected members of the public are protected by substantive restrictions in the ordinances, and they may also have input regarding a proposal at its public hearing. Regional or environmental interests are prominent examples of that type of stakeholder. With impetus from the federal government, states have adopted standards for environmental protection that may be incorporated directly into local ordinance by reference. Thus, protecting environmental interests is sometimes an integral part of a local approval process. However, because local ordinances may not require that affected members of the public receive notice, those likely to be impacted may have to take initiative to protect their interests. In New Jersey, affected members of the public have the same access to courts that neighbors have. In some states, though, those stakeholders must demonstrate that their interests would be impacted in some significant way different from that experienced by the general public.

The developer is the final stakeholder. The developer's interests are protected by a process that adheres to its own rules, prohibits what the ordinances proscribe, permits what is allowed, and reaches a decision within a reasonable period of time. The process imposes only those submission and time costs that are necessary or reasonable to ensure that all stakeholder interests are given due consideration. The developer also is guaranteed access to courts if aggrieved by the local decision.

FOUR SOURCES OF DELAY
IN THE REGULATORY PROCESS

Four elements determine the time needed to reach a final decision in a regulatory process. They are:

1. The complexity of the issues presented

2. The competence of the participants in addressing issues

3. The capacity of the constituent actors to process an application and perform their designated functions

4. The institutional structure of the process

Complexity

The larger a proposed project, the more potentially complex is its compliance with requirements to provide services (for example, on-site wastewater treatment or recreation), to mitigate off-site impacts, and even to conform with the general intent of the ordinances. The more environmentally sensitive a site, the greater the number of compliance issues that are raised. The more densely populated an area surrounding a site, the more complex the evaluation of possible off-site impacts that may require mitigation. Reviewers have to take more time to assess complex problems if they are to properly perform their function of protecting stakeholder interests.

Competence

The level of training and experience of all participants determines how quickly they can address and resolve the issues. Developers who are familiar with submission requirements and who actively gather information can avoid delay caused by postsubmission requests for additional data or clarification of unclear materials. Well-trained regulators familiar with their areas of responsibility should be able to review proposals promptly, know what information is necessary to ensure full compliance, sort through conflicting information with less uncertainty, and determine compliance more quickly. Board members familiar with ordinances and standards for conducting hearings and the exercise of discretion will need less time to receive input from stakeholders and will make fewer decisions that will be appealed either because the stakeholders are dissatisfied with the process or because the decision is not in accordance with the standards in the ordinances.

Capacity

No matter how well prepared the participants or the submissions, there will be unnecessary delays if there are too few appropriately trained individuals to process applications within the prescribed time.

Institutional Structure

As previously noted, each review or hearing that is held takes time, so adding levels of approval increases the time required for final approval. The institutional structure determines the number of reviews or hearings that must be held before a proposal receives final approval, and whether multiple approvals can be sought concurrently or must be obtained consecutively. Similarly, institutional structure determines the length of time required for a court to hear an appeal.

The academic literature on bureaucracy points to other possible sources of delay based on the motivations and self-interest of planners and public managers as well as the institutional structure. These include "bureaucratic delays" and "agenda delays."

ISSUES IN THE LOCAL REGULATORY PROCESS

State Delegation of Regulatory Authority

As in many states, zoning and the subdivision of land in New Jersey historically were regulated by incorporated municipalities, so-called home rule.[4] Home rule essentially delegated broad powers from Trenton to municipalities to regulate the use of land within their jurisdictions. Since 1969, however, that autonomy has been increasingly restricted by the state and its independent commissions, as well as by state court decisions. Today, land-use regulation in New Jersey is controlled by myriad government bodies, from the local to regional to state level. Thus, local authority to approve desired development has been substantially reduced. While the development of uses or projects rejected by a municipality cannot proceed, projects approved or desired by a municipality may be slowed or stopped by state or regional reviews or laws.

North Carolina has no home-rule provisions in either its state constitution or statutes. State government theoretically retains unfettered control over all municipalities: counties and incorporated cities and towns.

However, through legislative delegation, North Carolina has granted authority over the two basic forms of land development regulation—zoning and subdivision control—to its local governments. State law specifically provides that the legislative grant "shall be broadly construed and grants of power shall be construed to include any additional and supplementary powers that are reasonably necessary or expedient to carry them into execution and effect. . . ."[5] The delegation of authority is highly discretionary, conferring virtually complete power over zoning and the subdivision approval process on municipalities, with few limitations or requirements. Unlike New Jersey, North Carolina has not passed laws imposing substantial procedural requirements governing how municipalities review development applications, although there are some minor substantive limitations. With respect to environmental issues, the state has established performance standards but has left enforcement mostly at the local level. The state retains the right to intervene in development approval, to the point of reassuming the role of permit-granting authority, if local administration is not acceptable to the state regulators.

Local Development Approval in New Jersey

There are no unincorporated areas in New Jersey; there are 566 incorporated cities, boroughs, towns, villages, and townships. These municipalities vary in population from Newark's approximately 268,000 residents (based on 1998 Census Bureau estimates; U.S. Bureau of the Census 2000) to townships of fewer than 100. All of the municipalities exercise land-use control.

A series of laws enacted in the mid-1970s attempted to make local ordinances and approval procedures more uniform throughout the state. Among the most prominent of these were the New Jersey Uniform Construction Code and the New Jersey Municipal Land Use Law. The intent of these laws was to reduce local control over both substantive and procedural requirements of residential development permitting: Local communities would have less flexibility in shaping their ordinances to suit the interests and desires of the local population and reduced ability to use home-rule powers to either facilitate or hinder development. However, New Jersey municipalities have differed substantially in the processing of land-use approvals throughout the 1980s and 1990s (as evidenced in our survey results), lessening the impact of these laws in making outcomes more uniform.

The New Jersey Uniform Construction Code Act was signed into law in 1975 and implemented in 1977. The act brought all construction code adoption under the aegis of the state, although code enforcement is still carried out by municipalities. Currently, builders have a choice of building under one of two national codes, Building Officials and Code Administrators International, Inc. (BOCA) or, for one- and two-family houses, Council of American Building Officials (CABO).

The New Jersey Municipal Land Use Law (MLUL) was adopted in 1976. That act regularized the delegation of subdivision approval authority to municipalities to provide for more consistency in procedural requirements among jurisdictions. The act does not diminish local authority by dictating use as much as it prescribes procedures. Municipalities are charged, through planning boards, with creating municipal master plans and zoning ordinances governing height, bulk, coverage, setbacks, infrastructure, historic areas, shade trees, and other amenities. Except for a single-family home or duplex planned for a fully conforming lot, all site plans, including lot-line changes for existing subdivisions, must be approved by a planning board or a board of adjustment.

The planning boards consist of a municipality's mayor and six or eight individuals appointed by the mayor and the governing body. Those people prepare and adopt the municipal master plans and approve subdivisions, site plans, and bulk variances. Planning boards may grant variances from some substantive subdivision requirements, although their powers are limited. They may not grant use variances, allow deviation from specifications for conditional uses, or permit increases in permitted floor-area ratios, density, or height in excess of 10 feet or 10 percent of the maximum height specified. Zoning boards of adjustment decide whether to grant use variances; they also hear and decide appeals of enforcement decisions made by an administrative officer and requests for interpretations of zoning maps or ordinances. Finally, zoning boards of adjustment have authority to grant variances from zoning restrictions.

Municipalities are allowed some flexibility under the MLUL to establish approval standards, although many procedural limitations are specified in the statute. Communities may distinguish between minor and major subdivisions, allowing less-stringent review for the former. Typically, a minor subdivision requires no infrastructure improvements and is limited to four or fewer lots, although municipalities differ with respect to what may be considered a minor subdivision. Municipal ordinances determine what permits and exemption letters a developer must have in place prior to making application for either minor or major subdivisions. By state law, a municipality has forty-five days to decide on an application for a minor subdivision after submission of a completed application. If a municipality does not respond to a completed application within the stipulated time period, the application is automatically approved. Approvals for a minor subdivision are generally granted after only one meeting of a planning board, but developers of minor subdivisions still must secure any required county and state permits for soil erosion control, wetlands conservation, and so on.

All other subdivisions are major subdivisions, and securing approval for them is much more complex and time-consuming. As part of the application process for a major subdivision, all property owners within 200 feet of the subject property must be notified of the proposal. Before making a decision, the planning board must hold a public hearing at which arguments for and against the subdivision are presented. Under the MLUL, a municipality has ninety-five days from submission of a completed application to act on a major subdivision request. As with minor subdivisions, if a board fails to act within the stipulated time period, the application is automatically approved. Because boards often ask for time extensions and applicants sometimes require hearing postponements, major subdivision approvals often exceed that ninety-five day limit.

Preliminary plans submitted to a planning board for approval may be fully engineered plans, although, according to the MLUL, they need only be "in tentative form for discussion purposes."[6] Comments, usually in writing, are made by the planning board's professionals, and the planning board members themselves may study the entire set of plans. The developer may then modify the plans to address the comments and concerns expressed by the planners, resubmitting a revised set of preliminary plans for further discussion. That iterative process can continue for months before the final set of preliminary plans is submitted. In some municipalities, a concept plan review is used to allow an applicant to get a sense of how a proposed project will be reviewed before he or she spends resources on engineering, as well as to afford more opportunity for the planning board to provide input.

In addition to a planning board approval fee, an applicant must pay the fees of professionals and consultants the board uses in its evaluation of the application. (In larger municipalities, and in some undergoing rapid growth, those professionals are municipal employees; in other places, they are independent consultants.) Typically, these charges are estimated by the board's administrator, billed to the applicant, and placed in an escrow account maintained by the municipality for the benefit of the applicant.[7]

There are two types of subdivision approvals: *preliminary* and *final*. Preliminary approval gives an applicant the right to develop a subdivision within three years, although that authority may be extended for another two years (and under certain conditions, longer) upon application to the planning board. Preliminary approval may include planning board conditions that must be satisfied prior to final subdivision approval. After preliminary approval,[8] an applicant may proceed to final approval or commence installing improvements prior to final approval. After a final approval resolution is passed, an applicant typically posts a letter of credit or a performance bond with the municipality.

Final subdivision approval guarantees the developer that a municipality's terms and conditions for that approval will remain in effect for a period of two years, with the possibility of extensions granted by the planning board. Final subdivision approval is given when all conditions and improvements for the subdivision are completed (including either the building of infrastructure/improvements or providing a performance guarantee of 120 percent of the cost of installation of the infrastructure/improvements). The developer also must post a two-year maintenance guarantee bond after the municipality accepts the improvements.

In an effort to ensure uniformity among local ordinance requirements as well as an attempt to contain costs of infrastructure, the Uniform Site Standards Law was enacted in 1993; its regulations became effective June 3, 1997. By setting uniform technical standards for residential site improvements in all municipalities, it is expected to have an effect similar to that of the Uniform Construction Code Act.

Local Development Approval in North Carolina

There are 100 counties and 516 incorporated cities and towns in North Carolina, of which 244 have populations of less than 1,000. Only 45.6 percent of the state's population lives within an incorporated municipality. The largest city in the state, Charlotte, has an estimated 1998 population of 430,000, and only ten cities have populations exceeding 50,000.[9]

As in New Jersey, the state has delegated regulatory power to municipalities but with few of the substantive or procedural limitations imposed by the MLUL. Municipalities have used their power to dramatically different degrees. Only thirty-six of the 100 counties in North Carolina have adopted countywide zoning. Forty-seven have zoning over less than one-quarter of their jurisdictions, and thirty-two have no zoning. Twenty-four North Carolina counties have no subdivision ordinances. Those figures reflect the extent and dispersion of development in the state: The least-regulated counties tend to be the least developed. Of the rural mountain counties, 43 percent (ten of twenty-three) have no subdivision ordinances; 30 percent (seven of twenty-three) have no zoning. Within the Piedmont, the most intensely developed part of the state, 94 percent (thirty-two of thirty-four) of the counties have zoning, and 85 percent (twenty-nine of thirty-four) have subdivision ordinances.[10]

These subdivision ordinances may control the usual infrastructure components—street layouts, gutters, curbs and sidewalks, lighting—as well as amenities, such as easements, recreational facilities, and the reservation of school sites. A municipality may incorporate additional design restrictions, such as tree ordinances prohibiting the cutting of certain-size trees or landscaping requirements of visual buffers, into the ordinances. An ordinance may provide for fees in lieu for recreational facilities and roads. Dedication of rights-of-way may be required, and ordinances may also provide density bonuses or transferable development rights for dedicated rights-of-way.

Under delegated zoning power, municipalities regulate the size and height of buildings, the number of stories, lot coverage ratio, setbacks, open space, density, and use. The ordinances may be in the form of numerical requirements or performance standards.[11] Zoning districts may include "of right" and "conditional" uses and "conditional use" districts, the last requiring all uses to have specific approval by the permitting authority,[12] and overlay districts. City councils or boards of adjustment approve conditional (or special) uses and may impose "reasonable and appropriate conditions and safeguards."[13] The principal purpose for declaring an area a conditional-use district would be to allow a municipality and a developer to negotiate uses and conditions for a project that might not be allowable under any of the more conventional zoning district classifications.[14] Mixed-use zones, such as those for planned-unit developments (PUDs), are allowed.

Procedurally, local governments have used the discretion conferred upon them by the state to establish submission requirements for residential subdivisions. North Carolina specifies technical requirements only for recorded plats; a local governing body is free to require whatever else it deems necessary to evaluate a development proposal. An ordinance may require only an engineered plan showing lots and infrastructure, sufficient for compliance review, or may require developers to submit transportation impact reports, tree surveys, soil analyses, erosion control plans, stormwater calculations, landscape plans, landscape preservation plans, resource conservation district maps, topographic maps showing existing and proposed elevations, environmental impact statements, or other information as part of any subdivision application.

Municipalities also are free to specify the steps through which proposals are reviewed, because state statutes establish no specific process or time frames within which action is required. That flexibility has resulted in substantial variations in subdivision and rezoning requirements throughout the state, although the procedures generally follow the model discussed earlier in this chapter, wherein there is technical compliance review of a preliminary plan and final approval by elected officials. For PUD or "conditional zoning" approvals, a preliminary plan would be the preliminary master plan for the entire community, not plans for individual neighborhoods or pods.

A governing body, either a board of county commissioners or a city or town council, may delegate decision-making authority to a planning board or staff, or it may retain final authority for itself. Whether or not authority is delegated may depend on whether a proposed subdivision is "minor" or "major." Minor subdivisions—those containing fewer than a locally specified number of units—can be approved by a planning board or its staff. In Durham, for example, a minor subdivision contains fewer than fifty units; in Chapel Hill, a minor subdivision has fewer than five. Any development larger than that locally designated number must be approved by a town council.

Some jurisdictions in North Carolina use optional advisory boards that make recommendations to the decision-making authority. In places where they do exist, their power varies widely. Some locations require that applicants submit plans to an advisory board for a hearing and approval either concurrently or following compliance review. In some places, advisory board disapproval kills an application; in another, a board's comments are less important. Local ordinances may require that advisory boards hold public hearings, giving the public an opportunity to express itself, but again, hearings are not mandated by state law.

Requirements for hearings also differ. There may be numerous public hearings or none at all. Some communities require a full, well-publicized event; in other places, zoning issues are regular agenda items, and no one is given special notice.

A key variable in the approval process is the length of time necessary to secure a final decision. Many jurisdictions establish strict deadlines for committees and boards handling applications for development, with approval deemed granted if action is not taken as required. The timetable may include a schedule of meetings for all reviewing committees and boards based upon the date of the initial submission of the preliminary plan. Such schedules allow an applicant to know the action deadline for each step in the approval process. However, state law doesn't mandate any deadlines, and the board with final approval authority may have no deadline at all, which can result in long delays. Requests to change zoning follow procedural requirements similar to subdivision applications, with approval authority, notice and hearing requirements, and timetables differing substantially among jurisdictions. In some communities, zoning adjustments or variances are routinely approved; in others, they are granted only rarely. Public hearings may be mandated, or public meetings may suffice. Public opposition may have great or little influence over prospects for approval. For development proposals requiring both zoning and subdivision approval, a municipality may permit concurrent processing of both applications, or it may require that they be handled sequentially.

Zoning requests are generally submitted to the town's planning staff, which will pass them along to the board with a recommendation. A zoning board may have authority to approve or may add its recommendation, forwarding the request to a city council or county commission, which in turn may act at either a public hearing, with notice, or a public meeting, without specific notice that a request will be considered.

Incorporated cities and towns may exercise regulatory authority over their own territory and can decide unilaterally to extend their jurisdiction up to one mile outside corporate limits. By mutual agreement with the impacted county, an incorporated municipality may extend its jurisdiction up to three miles beyond its limits, or a county may regulate within the city limits. Joint governance agreements that allow a city to regulate are possible, subject to input from county commissioners. Counties have power over unincorporated areas not regulated by incorporated municipalities. In two North Carolina jurisdictions, Charlotte–Mecklenburg County and Durham–Durham County, city and county governments have merged their planning and regulatory apparatuses.[15]

The process described above is illustrated in figure 4, which shows the chain of events governing development permitting in Chapel Hill, North Carolina. The process is of average complexity. The town manager's office plays a central role in meeting with an applicant, managing the solicitation of reviews, and making recommendations to the planning board, which then makes recommendations to the town council. In Chapel Hill, four or more boards and several town departments may be involved: a board of adjustment, a design review board, the planning board, and one or several

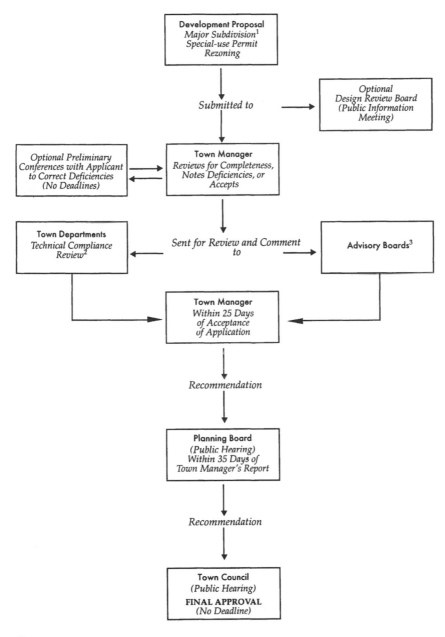

Notes:
1. One that creates more than four lots or dedicates or improves a new street.
2. Includes review by departments of planning, police, fire, public works, and recreation, as well as other town departments, as appropriate.
3. The advisory boards have responsibility for specific areas of concern, such as site design and traffic impacts. They hold public hearings before making their recommendations.

FIGURE 4
Development proposal review procedure—Town of Chapel Hill, North Carolina

advisory boards, as well as the town departments of planning, police, fire, public works, and recreation.

Summary

With respect to local permitting, New Jersey and North Carolina present some distinct contrasts. New Jersey's Municipal Land Use Law does not dictate land uses; it allows local discretion as to the location and types of development that occur. Yet by prescribing uniform planning procedures, MLUL and other related state acts arguably give New Jersey communities less flexibility in tailoring ordinances to particular preferences than their North Carolina counterparts enjoy. Municipalities in North Carolina have almost unlimited authority to adopt whatever kinds of substantive and procedural rules they desire.

The effect of the state limitations may be seen by contrasting the relative uniformity of New Jersey procedures with the widely varying procedural requirements operative in different places in North Carolina. While legal procedures in New Jersey appear to be relatively consistent from one municipality to another, they may vary somewhat in practice because state statutes do not entirely eliminate local discretion. North Carolina, where development is more desired and encouraged, allows communities to streamline the process to ensure that final decisions are rendered within relatively short periods of time. That flexibility, however, may result in an approval process that mandates expensive submissions, has no final deadline for actions, is filled with opportunities for delay, and contains few clear criteria upon which the final decision must be based. The choice is within the discretion of each community.

Other points for comparison between North Carolina and New Jersey concern the fiscal and political structures that reinforce the importance of local land-use and development decisions. Interestingly, both states have roughly 600 counties and municipalities (New Jersey has 21 counties and 566 municipalities; North Carolina has 100 counties and 524 municipalities). Many of the jurisdictions in each state are small in population (about 450 of New Jersey's 566 municipalities had fewer than 20,000 people in 1990) and land area (more than half the New Jersey municipalities are fewer than five square miles in area). Thus, both states are carved into many political jurisdictions and have various responsibilities for local services.

One main difference between the two states is that North Carolina still has considerable expanses of unincorporated area. In these places, and in small incorporated municipalities with few governmental resources, development is subject only to county regulation, which tends to be relatively weak. Indeed, many counties do not have zoning ordinances at all.

Another difference is that New Jersey has almost four times as many school districts as does North Carolina, and its schools rely more heavily on local property taxes. The effect of growth on schools and the issue of who pays for education have more local impact on New Jersey localities than those in North Carolina.

ISSUES IN THE STATE AND REGIONAL APPROVAL PROCESS

In addition to the local approvals needed for residential projects, developers frequently must secure permits or waivers from other levels of government or agencies, particularly where there may be environmental impacts. Those requirements are usually driven by federal and/or state laws.

As in all states, New Jersey and North Carolina land use and development are subject to federal regulations. The authority of both the Army Corps of Engineers and the United States Environmental Protection Agency extends throughout the states and affects many proposed development projects. In some instances, a federal agency administers an act directly; in others, it sets performance standards and makes the states responsible for enforcement. It may also allow some states to administer federal regulations upon certification of compliance with agency requirements. In 1994, for example, the New Jersey Department of Environmental Protection assumed authority from the federal government for administering the Freshwater Wetlands Program. Other federal programs, such as the Endangered Species Act and the Comprehensive Environmental Response Compensation and Liability Act, have appreciable impact on land use and development in both New Jersey and North Carolina, just as they do in other states.

New Jersey

New Jersey has programs for soil erosion, floodplain management, water quality management, air quality management, solid waste disposal, extension of sewer lines, traffic and transportation management, farmland preservation, wetlands conservation, affordable housing, and others. Just as the federal government sometimes sets standards but leaves enforcement to the states, New Jersey delegates some programs to localities. Several, such

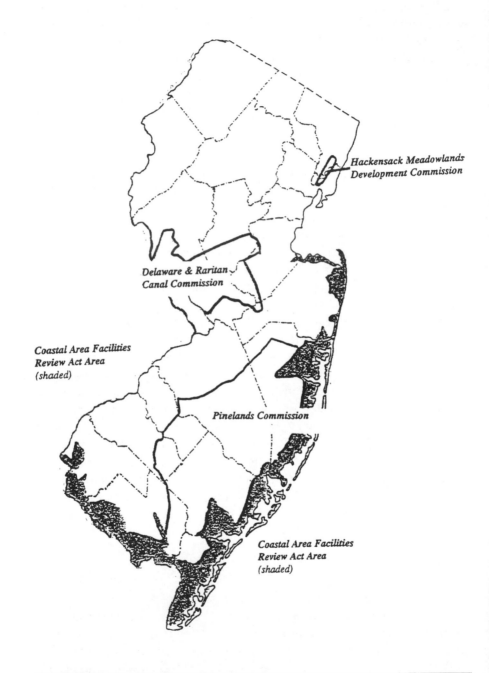

FIGURE 5
New Jersey's regional regulatory authorities

as soil erosion and sediment control, are managed at the county or regional level under state direction. Others are administered directly by the state agency issuing the regulations, most often the New Jersey Department of Environmental Protection (DEP). Still others may be locally controlled in some jurisdictions and state run in others.

When a development proposal concerns a regulated area, a separate permit may be needed, frequently one having its own submission requirements and decision criteria, possibly with public hearings and opportunity for appeals. The New Jersey Municipal Land Use Law does not allow planning boards to require prior approvals or letters of nonapplicability, but some municipalities ignore those provisions. The actual building of a subdivision, including roads, homes, driveway openings, stormwater management, wells, septic systems, and sewers, may also be subject to ordinances, approvals, and permits. Indeed, roads, stormwater management, and sewers all became subject to statewide site standards when the Residential Site Improvement Standards went into effect on June 3, 1996.

Regional Regulatory Bodies

In addition to state agencies, New Jersey has created regional agencies for various areas, giving them power over land uses within their respective jurisdictions. The regulatory bodies cover approximately 40 percent of the state's land area, as shown in figure 5. The state established the first regional regulatory entity, the Hackensack Meadowlands Development Commission, in 1969. It was created to protect 21,000 acres of meadowlands and to prepare a master plan for their development. The Commission's jurisdictional area includes municipalities in Bergen and Hudson Counties (see figure 5), and its authority supersedes any municipal regulation.

The Coastal Area Facility Review Act (CAFRA)[16] was enacted in 1973. CAFRA requires a permit to build certain types of developments in the coastal area (see figure 5). Any development in the CAFRA region must conform to both municipal and CAFRA requirements.

In 1974 New Jersey created the Delaware and Raritan Canal Commission. It was authorized to develop a master plan and to review all projects to determine their impact on the Delaware and Raritan Canal Park. The area of the commission's review covers 400 square miles spanning thirty-five municipalities in five counties (see figure 5).

The Pinelands Protection Act of 1979 created the Pinelands Commission to preserve and maintain the character of the Pinelands—which comprises approximately 20 percent of the state—and to protect and maintain water quality while encouraging appropriate development. Those local municipal master plans and land-use ordinances within the Pinelands jurisdiction must be certified by the Pinelands Commission.

In addition, there are three scenic-river regional regulatory authorities and three metropolitan planning organizations involved with regional transportation planning. Those organizations currently are not very involved with land use as it relates to housing.

The members of all these commissions are appointed by the governor and confirmed by the state senate. And although the Commissioner of the Department of Community Affairs chairs the Hackensack Meadowlands Development Commission, the regional regulatory authorities act with very little state oversight.

The procedural impact of the regional regulatory authorities is generally the same as it is with state agencies. Developers may be required to secure additional approvals beyond those from local bodies, entailing more submissions and hearings. Even where a governing regional authority does not require a permit, local governments may require certification of non-applicability or a specific waiver from the authority before considering a development application. Consistency is often an issue when developers require approvals from the commissions and multiple state governments (for example, DEP for wetlands and stream encroachment).[17]

The Mount Laurel Decisions

Not all state intervention in local land-use control has been from the legislature; the state courts have played a noteworthy role in New Jersey. In early 1975, the New Jersey Supreme Court's Mount Laurel I[18] decision obligated municipalities to provide zoning for their fair share of their region's affordable housing needs. The New Jersey Supreme Court later noted in Mount Laurel II[19] that the decision was effective not in producing housing but in providing work for lawyers and planners.

The 1983 Mount Laurel II decision included a provision for the "builder's remedy," which encouraged builders to sue any municipality with a zoning ordinance that failed to afford an opportunity for the "appropriate variety and choice of housing" necessary to meet the municipality's fair share of the low- and moderate-income housing needed in the region. The decision put the burden of proof on municipalities; they would be required to show that their zonings were not exclusionary.

Municipalities perceived the *Mount Laurel II* decision as a major infringement on their right of self-determination. Not wanting to see builders or the courts determine the direction of development in their communities, but expecting to be required to implement the Court's decision, they clamored for state help. In response to *Mount Laurel II*, the Fair Housing Act was enacted in 1985, and the State Planning Act was passed in 1986.

The Fair Housing Act created the New Jersey Council on Affordable Housing (COAH), charged with determining a municipality's present and prospective "fair share" of regional housing needs. The State Planning Act was enacted in part to address the issue of determining the areas where new affordable housing would be needed.

The State Planning Act of 1986

The State Planning Act of 1986 created the Office of State Planning and a state planning commission. It further directed the state planning commission to prepare and adopt an advisory plan for statewide planning and development every three years. According to the act, these plans would protect historic and cultural areas, preserve open space and recreational properties, favor urban centers for development and redevelopment in promoting economic growth, and provide adequate public services and housing at a reasonable cost. All levels of government would use these plans to ensure sound, integrated planning.

From the beginning, the state planning commission promoted a concept of "communities of place." Such communities are conceived as ideal for living and working: They are human in scale, with an easily accessible central core of commercial and community services, and they are dynamic, diverse, compact, and efficient. They have unique characters, charm, and integrity that proponents hope will lead to healthier cities, a cleaner environment, and a robust economy.

The State Planning Act directed the state planning commission to solicit and consider the plans, comments, and advice of county, municipal, and other local and regional agencies. The county planning boards were authorized to "negotiate plan cross-acceptance" between the local planning bodies within their counties, thereby assuring that local, county, and state plans would be compatible. Those efforts resulted in the first New Jersey State Development and Redevelopment Plan, which was produced in 1989 and adopted in 1992.

New Jersey Summary

The regulatory environment in New Jersey combines elements common to many states. For example, there is a delegation of zoning and subdivision activity to local government, with oversight by regional regulatory authorities. There are also the more unique requirements of the *Mount Laurel* system of "fair share" housing allocations. Critics of the complexity of the New Jersey regulatory environment claim that equally effective safeguards of rational development could be accomplished with less procedurally burdensome regulations. Supporters contend that New Jersey is a particularly complex state. It is partially included in two of the largest metropolitan areas in the country (New York and Philadelphia), with resulting development pressures. There are unique historic preservation concerns in many areas, as well as a variety of environmental constraints that act as a brake on some development initiatives. New Jersey's regulatory environment may be complex, but so are the social, cultural, and environmental contexts within which development occurs.

North Carolina

The state's role in wastewater management, floodplain protection, erosion and sedimentation control, watershed protection, the environmental impact assessment process, and coastal area management is nominally the same in New Jersey and North Carolina. However, our interviews suggest some important differences in practice. We summarize the North Carolina case here, then provide more detail in chapter 6, where we compare survey results for the two states.

North Carolina seems to have struck a good balance between allowing local discretion and maintaining strong central control in environmental protection. Local discretion is possible because the state provides clear rules and maintains a strong presence in the enforcement area. The lines of authority between the state and its municipalities seem to be well understood.

The exercise of state power takes a variety of forms. State statutes set standards or decision criteria, and state agencies have rule-making authority. In almost all environmental areas, the state agency has authority to intervene directly in the local administration of the rules if the agency determines that a municipality is not performing satisfactorily.

Following the pattern of federal environmental laws, the state mandates performance standards and then delegates responsibility for meeting those standards to local governments. (Those state standards are typically driven by federal requirements, such as the Clean Water Act.) Municipal ordinances must conform to the state mandates, with limited local discretion in administration and enforcement. However, local governments may impose more stringent limitations than the state, if they choose, with state agency approval of local ordinance provisions.[20]

The delegation of authority is complicated by the presence of both incorporated municipalities and counties. The state may give a county authority to administer state regulations within the limits of incorporated municipalities, resulting in an added governmental authority in the permitting process.

The lines of authority in permitting provide a case in point. As in New Jersey, permitting in North Carolina is fragmented among local, regional, and state governments. For environmental interests, the state or regional level establishes standards, with enforcement at either the local or higher level. However, municipalities in North Carolina have more flexibility in shaping the parts of the permitting process over which they have authority. They can establish submission requirements, set their own timetables for approvals, and delegate final approval power to staff. For communities favoring residential development, that freedom can allow speedy action on applications, with little public input.

4

Regulation and Residential Development in Practice

The outcomes of the regulatory process described in the preceding chapter may deviate from what legislators and regulators intended when drafting statutes, ordinances, and rules. For example, as we suggested, staff shortages tend to create delays in application reviews. In addition, we suggested that multiple reviews at different levels of government attenuate a permitting timeline and may lead to inconsistent discretionary requirements. Then, too, regulators who are given some flexibility—ostensibly to accommodate a wide range of sound proposals—sometimes use it to deny or delay projects that, although in technical compliance, may not meet the spirit of the rules. Similarly, public hearings and court appeals, intended in part to ensure that government officials follow the rules, are also powerful tools for opponents of development. Foes can use hearings to politicize an approval process and convince elected officials not to follow the rules or to delay or kill projects.

To obtain a better understanding of the differences between intended and actual regulatory practice in New Jersey and North Carolina, we surveyed regulators (engineers and planners) and developers in both states. (See Appendix II for more information on our survey and methodology.) The response of regulators was higher in North Carolina than in New Jersey. Of 150 forms mailed to officials in New Jersey, thirty-four were returned (a response rate of 22.6 percent). In North Carolina, sixty-five (52 percent) of 125 regulator forms were returned. Not every form was completed, however. Moreover, many of the North Carolina respondents worked in areas without zoning ordinances; therefore, the usable number of responses for any one question was often lower than the total number of forms returned. Nonetheless, the questionnaires enabled us to contrast observations and insights from stakeholders with different perspectives. The questions concerned the operation of the existing system as well as possible changes that might make the process function more efficiently. We also conducted case studies to provide information about regulatory practice in specific contexts.

DELAYS DUE TO REQUESTS FOR WAIVERS AND VARIANCES

No set of rules can address every possible contingency in every proposal; thus, virtually all ordinances affecting development have provisions for waivers, special exceptions, and/or variances. Sometimes exceptions to written requirements are necessary or desirable—perhaps to allow an innovative project that may not meet all mandates, or which may accomplish regulatory objectives better than a complying design; to avoid a taking; or for some other legitimate reason.

From a developer's perspective, variances and waivers may be used either to avoid complying with regulatory restrictions that could be prohibitively expensive or to allow more-profitable developments that might not be permitted under the letter of existing rules. Because obtaining relief takes time and money, there are risks for any developer who might need or choose to seek a change.

The surveys reveal that New Jersey developers request variances or waivers for subdivision, zoning, and both local and state environmental regulations much more frequently than their North Carolina counterparts (table 3).

Requests for such exceptions to the rules add to the time needed to secure approvals. New Jersey developers gave twelve months as the median time to secure approval of a subdivision ordinance waiver, with the average time being sixteen months. For rezonings, the median time for approval was fourteen months, with an average of twenty-nine months. For both types of relief, developers thought a time frame of four-and-a-half months for a final decision was reasonable. Regulators were asked about the maximum number of days allowed under applicable ordinances from initial submission to final approval for subdivisions of more than

TABLE 3

Regulators' Responses: Frequency of Requests
for Waivers or Variances

Category	New Jersey						North Carolina					
	RARELY		SOMETIMES		FREQUENTLY		RARELY		SOMETIMES		FREQUENTLY	
	%	n	%	n	%	n	%	n	%	n	%	n
SUBDIVISION	22.7	5	22.7	5	54.5	12	65.0	26	25.0	10	10.0	4
ZONING	34.8	8	34.8	8	30.4	7	58.1	25	32.6	14	9.3	4

Source: Authors' calculations from survey document responses

twenty-five lots (with and without requests for waivers) for zoning changes, and for site plan approval. Their responses are shown in table 4.

One interesting observation is not reflected in the table: In both states, the number of days regulators report as allowable for review is significantly higher than the figure developers perceived. That distinction reflects the different perspectives of developers and regulators. Developers tend to focus on statutory time requirements, which are usually less than sixty days; regulators understand that statutory time limits for any form of discretionary action, in land use or otherwise, are easily circumvented. A decision-making board can simply indicate that it will deny an application unless it is granted an extension for further consideration. A request for extension is usually accompanied by a request for additional information from, or studies by, the applicant. If the applicant does not comply, the board can deny the application for failure to submit requisite information— a pretext that will withstand an appeal, or at worst, merely draw a remand. In such a situation, an applicant has little choice but to agree to an extension. The maximum number of days allowed for review, therefore, is really much more than what is specified in statutes.

Second, table 4 demonstrates one impact of the difference in local control over procedural aspects of permitting allowed under the New Jersey MLUL compared to North Carolina practice. The median time allowed in New Jersey, except for zoning changes, is consistently higher than in North Carolina, but the maximum is significantly lower. The range of times allowed for decision making is much narrower in New Jersey, showing more consistency in the procedural requirements of New Jersey communities.

TABLE 4

Regulators' Responses: Time Allowed
for Applicable Ordinances

Category	New Jersey			North Carolina		
	MAXIMUM DAYS ALLOWED	MEDIAN DAYS ALLOWED	AVERAGE DAYS ACTUALLY TAKEN	MAXIMUM DAYS ALLOWED	MEDIAN DAYS ALLOWED	AVERAGE DAYS ACTUALLY TAKEN
	n	n	n	n	n	n
Subdivision with waivers	165 20	120 20	21 9	365 24	58 24	15 37
Subdivision, no waivers	120 20	53 20	21 9	365 27	45 27	12 40
Zoning changes	90 5	45 5	20 15	270 19	60 19	27 38
Site plan review	120 18	53 18	21 19	180 21	30 21	5 39

Source: Authors' calculations from survey document responses

The third notable observation is that an actual technical review by regulators (planning and engineering staffs, for example) is not a time-consuming process. The one- to five-week time frame noted in the table is counted from the time a plan is received in a regulator's office to the time it is returned to the applicant.[21]

The reasons for delay in processing applications are numerous. When asked to rate what led to delay in approval of subdivision applications, regulators in New Jersey and North Carolina, as well as developers in New Jersey, rated the factors in table 5 as major contributors. The table allows comparison between regulators in the two states as well as between developers and regulators in New Jersey.

The first difference obvious from the table is the degree to which each group perceives the other to be responsible for delaying subdivision approval. In New Jersey, developers were inclined to believe that regulators' lack of training or understanding of the issues was a major factor, while regulators were more likely to cite developer error.

Beyond that assignment of blame, a substantial percentage of regulators and developers in New Jersey believed that excessively long review

TABLE 5

Reasons for Delay in Acting on Subdivision Applications

Reason for Delay	Percentage of Respondents Indicating Reason for Delay					
	NEW JERSEY DEVELOPERS		NEW JERSEY REGULATORS		NORTH CAROLINA REGULATORS	
	%	n	%	n	%	n
Organized citizen opposition	8.5	12	54.2	13	37.0	17
Individual/isolated opposition	14.9	21	8.3	2	8.7	4
Regulators' lack of training or understanding of issues	17.0	24	4.2	1	8.7	4
Allowable review periods longer than necessary	34.0	48	25.0	6	2.2	1
Inadequate staffing	10.6	15	16.7	4	30.4	14
Consultant, contractor, or developer error	2.1	3	45.8	11	32.7	16
Delays in negotiations	12.9	18	16.7	4	14.0	7

Source: Authors' calculations from survey document responses

periods were a major factor in delaying subdivision approvals. That is consistent with the data in table 4, which show that the average time regulators report using to review various types of applications is substantially below the median time allowed under applicable ordinances.

Regulators also cited organized opposition as a major factor in delay much more frequently than developers did. Since that dynamic is most noticeable in public hearings, where the public has a chance to influence elected decision makers, the potential for delay would be related to the number of hearings required. That regulators notice the effects of public opposition more than developers is not surprising. Regulators attend more hearings and work on a more regular basis with the decision-making boards; therefore, they are more likely to be aware of the extent to which board members might be swayed by the prospect of a large number of constituents organizing against a specific development proposal.

The surveys posed the same question concerning applications for zoning relief. The responses, shown in table 6, report the percentage of

TABLE 6

Reasons for Delay in Acting on Zoning Relief

Reason for Delay	Percentage of Respondents Indicating Reason for Delay					
	NEW JERSEY DEVELOPERS		NEW JERSEY REGULATORS		NORTH CAROLINA REGULATORS	
	%	n	%	n	%	n
Organized citizen opposition	21.8	17	66.7	16	59.1	26
Individual/isolated opposition	14.2	11	12.5	3	18.2	8
Regulators' lack of training or understanding of issues	19.2	15	12.5	3	6.8	3
Allowable review periods longer than necessary	21.8	17	8.3	2	2.3	1
Inadequate staffing	8.9	7	1.2	3	20.5	9
Consultant, contractor, or developer error	5.2	4	37.5	9	34.1	15
Delays in negotiations	8.9	7	25.0	6	22.7	10

Source: Authors' calculations from survey document responses

respondents who considered the reason listed as a major contributing factor in delaying final decisions. As with waivers of subdivision requirements, a significant percentage of both regulators and developers seem to consider the other group's inadequacies or errors a major cause of delay. Beyond that, more than half of all regulators, as well as one-fifth of developers, cited organized citizen opposition as a major factor in delaying zoning change approvals. That differs slightly from subdivision approvals, for which citizen opposition was listed as a major factor by smaller percentages of all groups.

The consistency with which regulators viewed organized citizen opposition as affecting the time lines of development approvals demonstrates the impact of requirements for public hearings. It is at public hearings that elected decision makers may be swayed; one planning board member calls that phenomenon "listening to taxpayers."

Compared to subdivision approvals, fewer regulators in New Jersey listed inadequate staffing as a major factor in delay of rezoning requests.

DELAYS DUE TO ENVIRONMENTAL PERMITS

The pattern of responses seems to shift with regard to environmental regulations. The percentages of respondents citing the reasons listed as major factors in delaying environmental permit approvals are shown in table 7.

TABLE 7

Reasons for Delay in Granting Environmental Permits

Reason for Delay	Percentage of Respondents Indicating Reason for Delay					
	NEW JERSEY DEVELOPERS		NEW JERSEY REGULATORS		NORTH CAROLINA REGULATORS	
	%	n	%	n	%	n
Organized citizen opposition	7.1	8	63.6	14	34.2	13
Individual/isolated opposition	5.4	6	9.1	2	13.2	5
Regulators' lack of training or understanding of issues	21.4	24	27.3	6	7.9	3
Allowable review periods longer than necessary	33.0	37	22.7	5	5.3	2
Inadequate staffing	20.6	23	27.3	6	28.9	11
Consultant, contractor, or developer error	3.6	4	31.8	7	28.9	11
Delays in negotiations	8.9	10	18.2	4	13.2	5

Source: Authors' calculations from survey document responses

In New Jersey, comparable percentages of developers and regulators mention regulators' lack of training, excessively long review periods, and inadequate staffing as major contributors to permitting delays. That response pattern is particularly noteworthy considering that the percentage of regulators who believe the complexity of the issues raised in environmental permitting is a major factor in causing delay is lower than for either

TABLE 8

Number of Approvals and Length of Time Needed for Environmental Permits in New Jersey

Type of Environmental Regulation	Mean Number of Jurisdictional Approvals Needed		Mean Number of Months to Obtain Approval		Mean Number of Months Approval Should Take	
		n		n		n
Wetlands	2.8	30	12.3	37	3.7	38
Critical areas/coastal zone management	2.5	7	11	7	2	8
Stream encroachment	2.1	22	7.3	25	2.3	25
Stormwater management	2.1	27	6.6	27	2.0	27
Sedimentation and soil erosion	1.7	36	4.3	36	1.6	6
Sewer/treatment works	2.8	15	9.1	14	3.1	12

Source: Authors' calculations from survey document responses

subdivision or zoning change approvals. Lack of adequate staffing in Trenton (the state capital), also cited as a factor in the case studies reported in this book, is caused, in part, by New Jersey funding cuts.

As was the case with both subdivision and zoning change approvals, developers in New Jersey consistently thought approvals took longer than necessary for all categories of environmental regulations, as shown in table 8.

One possible explanation for the length of time needed to review environmental permits is that regulating potential environmental impacts is more technically complex than regulating subdivisions and zoning matters. However, as shown in table 9, a smaller percentage of regulators responding to our survey considered complexity a major factor for delay in considering environmental permitting than for either subdivision or zoning applications. The mean of 2.8 for the number of jurisdictional approvals needed for wetlands regulation (table 8) is interesting, since Section 30 of the Freshwater Wetlands Protection Act mandates that the New Jersey Department of Environmental Protection (DEP) is the only agency that can consider wetlands regulation. That suggests respondents perceive multiple reviews within DEP.

TABLE 9

Is Complexity a Reason for Delays?

Complexity of Issues A Major Factor in Delaying Approval for:	Percentage of Respondents Agreeing			
	NEW JERSEY REGULATORS		NORTH CAROLINA REGULATORS	
	%	n	%	n
Subdivision applications	58.3	14	32.0	9
Zoning change requests	54.2	13	36.4	16
Environmental permits	45.5	10	31.6	12

Source: Authors' calculations from survey document responses

The data in table 9 seem to indicate that those reviewing submissions consider environmental issues to be slightly less complex than issues in other types of applications.

DELAYS DUE TO OVERLAPPING REGULATORY JURISDICTIONS

One clear difference between environmental permitting and either subdivision or zoning change approvals is that the latter are strictly the province of local government, whereas the former may involve permits from local, regional, and state agencies. Seventy-five percent of the New Jersey developers who responded to our survey strongly agreed with the statement that multiple approvals slowed the process, and another 16 percent agreed somewhat. Interestingly, as shown in table 8, the mean time needed to obtain approvals increases in relation to the number of jurisdictional approvals required. That is consistent with the belief that each additional required review adds to the total time needed for full approval of a project.

One factor in determining the time needed for environmental approvals is staffing levels—in other words, the capacity of a reviewing body to process applications. As we can see by comparing the data in tables 5, 6, and 7, inadequate staffing is cited by 20.6 percent of developers and 27.3

TABLE 10

Necessity of Multiple Reviews

Multiple Levels of Government Approvals Are Not Necessary to Achieve Substantive Regulatory Objectives:	Percentage of Respondents Agreeing			
	NEW JERSEY REGULATORS		NORTH CAROLINA REGULATORS	
	%	n	%	n
Subdivision applications	70.8	17	67.4	29
Zoning change requests	62.5	15	82.5	33
Environmental permits	66.7	16	52.6	20

Source: Authors' calculations from survey document responses

percent of regulators in New Jersey as a major factor in delaying applications (table 7). Those percentages, particularly for regulators, are significantly higher than those pertaining to either subdivision or zoning change approvals. Forty percent of the responding New Jersey regulators believed that increased staffing would be effective in reducing delays, and 32 percent thought it would be somewhat effective. Those sentiments were shared by the New Jersey DEP personnel who were interviewed.

Lengthy reviews resulting from multilayered regulation would not be considered "unnecessary" if they were needed to meet substantive regulatory objectives. Regulators in New Jersey and North Carolina were asked to what extent it was necessary to have multiple levels of government regulating the same general issue in order to achieve substantive (rather than procedural) objectives in different regulatory spheres. The percentages of those who rated multilayered regulation as unnecessary are shown in table 10.

The results shown in this table are consistent with regulators' responses to a question regarding measures that might be effective in reducing unnecessary delays in permitting: 54 percent of New Jersey regulators indicated that less regulatory overlap would be effective, and another 29 percent responded that it would be somewhat effective.[22]

SUMMARY

The survey responses shed some light on the reasons for delays in the regulatory process in New Jersey; however, there are no strong patterns. Different actors (in this case, regulators and developers) typically cite different reasons. The reasons for delay given by both parties range from New Jersey developers' tendency to ask for a relatively large number of waivers to inadequate staffing and overlapping authority requiring multiple reviews. The causes of delay generally differ according to regulatory area.

Of all the potential reasons for delay, we are most interested in those that can be addressed administratively or by changing the institutional structure. For example, inadequate staffing is cited as a leading source of delay in environmental permitting but not in the subdivision and zoning processes. Similarly, regulators' lack of training is cited more frequently for environmental than other types of regulation—not surprising, considering the relative complexity of environmental reviews.

A related problem with an administrative solution is the prevalence of errors in the material submitted for review, or in the review process itself. When asked what percentage of applications were returned because of minor technical or clerical errors after more than half the review period had elapsed, the median response by developers/builders was 10 percent, with a quarter of respondents answering 20 percent or higher. That is consistent with regulators' perceptions, shown in tables 5, 6, and 7, that developer error was a significant factor in delay. Forty-six percent of New Jersey regulators strongly agreed that more thorough screening by regulators at the time of submission would reduce the number of applications being returned, while 61 percent agreed strongly with the statement that regulators should be responsible for detecting such errors and that fees should include the cost of checking an application at the time it is submitted. One way of reducing the number of submission errors might be to make both application format and required information more consistent. Of regulators who responded in New Jersey, 44 percent thought such a measure would be effective in reducing unnecessary delay.

Another aspect of the institutional structure, the length of time allowed for review, drew different reactions from developers and regulators in New Jersey. Although a higher percentage of developers cited excessively long review periods as a cause of unnecessary delay, a significant number of regulators agreed with that perception with respect to both subdivisions and environmental permitting. When asked if shortening the review period would be effective in reducing unnecessary delay, 20 percent thought it would, whereas 12 percent responded that it would be somewhat effective. While the data in table 4 clearly indicate that the average time needed to review is considerably less than what is allowed, the length of a review period provided by ordinance must accommodate all applications, not just the average. In addition, deadlines are easy to circumvent; therefore, efforts to speed up application processing through shortened review periods may be ineffective in practice. Finally, the time needed to review is partially dependent upon staffing levels. More expeditious review might require more personnel.

One other institutional problem that appears to cause delays, especially with respect to environmental permitting, is shown in table 8: the existence of overlapping jurisdictions that require applicants to seek multiple approvals. If review could be streamlined within an agency (for example, DEP) and agreements were struck so that one of several agencies would take full responsibility for a review (for example, between regional authorities and DEP), the process would be less time-consuming. That "one-stop shopping" is more common in North Carolina than in New Jersey.

5

The Cost and Incidence of Regulation

The preceding chapters identified several types of regulatory costs. This chapter attempts to attach a monetary value to those costs and determine who ultimately pays them—developers in lower profits, landowners in reduced selling prices for the land, or home buyers in higher sales prices. We present three types of evidence: an analysis of survey responses by builders/developers and local planners and engineers in two states; statistical modeling of new building permits, using economic data and response data to form indices of regulatory strictness; and extensive case studies.

That three-pronged approach is essential, given the limitations of any single method. Any survey is subject to response bias and representativeness; our survey was particularly suspect given the strong self-interest of the respondent groups. In addition, our survey, as with every other study that surveys builders, suffered from low response rates.[23] Second, as previously noted, econometric analyses that attempt to explain sales price variation in terms of housing characteristics, including the extent of local regulation (what is called hedonic estimation), implicitly assume that all costs of regulation are borne by home buyers. That may be true in the long run, but our evidence indicates that it does not generally apply in the short run. Finally, case studies are illuminating but are of limited generalizability.

Our intention is to draw additive inferences from each of these approaches. If the results from each approach are generally consistent, a clear picture about regulatory costs emerges. Our overall conclusions are:

65

- [ ] The costs associated with regulation are sizable.

- [ ] Some of those costs are necessary to achieve agreed-upon goals (e.g., environmental protection), but others are unnecessary.

- [ ] Regulatory strictness is a matter of concern to builders/developers, so they often bypass places where regulations are perceived to be most burdensome, rapidly driving up housing costs in those locations.

- [ ] Generally, developers in less-regulated places are able to earn more profits than they can in more-regulated locations; however, extensive regulation has created opportunities for well-capitalized and savvy developers who build particular types of houses.

- [ ] A related observation is that the low end of the market suffers more from regulatory burden than does the high end; the building that continues at the lower end is by niche builders, operating in limited geographic areas.

- [ ] No general pattern applies to the short-run incidence of costs, which depends on local housing and land markets, idiosyncratic circumstances, and the abilities of developers. In the long run, however, consumers bear the burden since lower profits mean less building, and lower land prices mean less land will be converted to residential use.

- [ ] In the long run, regulatory costs are passed forward to consumers with a multiplier. Every dollar of costs, from regulation or other sources, translates into several dollars at the point of sale. The size of the multiplier varies from place to place and over time.

- [ ] There is more than a dollar-for-dollar translation of regulatory costs into final housing prices. The extent of that translation will vary from project to project depending on local conditions, the size of the house, land-to-structures ratio, and more.

We expand on these conclusions in this chapter.

SURVEY RESPONSES

We mailed 850 questionnaires to a stratified sample of builders/developers in New Jersey. Two hundred were sent a short version; 650 received a longer version. The long form went to builders/developers in each of four regions: the New York commuting shed; the Route 1 corridor; the Philadelphia commuting shed; and elsewhere in the state. (See Appendix II for a discussion of our survey methodology, sampling strategy, and validity issues.) Our initial response rate was low (approximately 12 percent), so we expanded our sample size for the short form by 300 (in addition to several hundred duplicate questionnaires sent again to the original sample). To increase the amount of data for the analysis, we conducted limited phone interviews with 77 additional builders/developers in New Jersey, drawn from the same sampling frame. We also sent 350 short questionnaires to builders/developers in North Carolina.

The number of usable completed responses was fewer than 250 in New Jersey and fewer than 50 in North Carolina. The number of responses on individual questions was often much lower. That response rate was less than what we had hoped to achieve and limits our ability to cross-tabulate the results by respondent characteristics. We have noted the number of respondents in each case.

The most direct approach to determining the perceived cost of delays was to ask builders/developers how different types of regulations affected their development costs. The answers they provided reflect both substantive and procedural costs, or what we classified in chapter 1 as *opportunity costs of restricted land use, hard costs, soft costs, out-of-pocket fees*, as well as *opportunity costs from delays*.

Table 11 lists the costs for subdivision requirements. The most costly subdivision requirements are interior streets and open space set-asides. Both the cost of providing infrastructure and the delay in securing approvals are factored into the difference between what a developer is willing to pay for raw versus improved land. The same type of data for zoning is shown in Table 12. Table 13 sets forth the responses for environmental regulations.

The most costly environmental regulations are coastal zone management restrictions, followed closely by wetlands restrictions. Both these sets of regulations reduce the developable land in a project, so that fixed project costs must be allocated over fewer units. The items in table 13 are mixed as to the degree to which they are commonly considered essential. In the questionnaire, we asked only how costly it was per unit to meet a specified requirement. Clearly some of the expenditures, regardless of cost, are essential for health, safety, environmental quality, or general welfare.

The regulations require additional reviews by the Department of Environmental Protection. Table 14 shows the average review times for several types of permits from July 1994 to December 1995. The table is part of a semiannual report of permit activities.

TABLE 11

Itemized Effects of Subdivision Requirements in New Jersey

Regulation Type	Median Cost per Unit ($)	Number of Respondents
Interior streets	$ 5,000	17
Curbs and gutters	1,000	16
Sidewalks	1,000	18
Water main	2,000	17
Sanitary sewers	2,400	17
Storm sewers	2,300	16
Landscaping	1,000	21
Street trees	500	15
Street lighting	275	10
Underground utility lines	900	14
Negotiated open space	3,500	12
Other	2,250	12
TOTAL	$22,125	

Source: Authors' calculations from survey document responses

TABLE 12

Itemized Effects of Zoning Regulations in New Jersey

Regulation Type	Median Cost per Unit ($)	Number of Respondents
Street-width requirements	$1,000	8
Lot-width requirements	3,000	9
Restrictions on clustering	2,000	7
Steep-slope restrictions	100	5
Bond-release difficulties	500	11
Discretionary planning-board decisions	1,000	11
Other	2,000	1
TOTAL	$9,600	

Source: Authors' calculations from survey document responses

TABLE 13

Itemized Effects of Environmental Regulations in New Jersey

Regulation Type	Median Cost per Unit ($)	Number of Respondents
Wetlands	$1,750	20
Critical areas/coastal zone management	1,800	8
Stream encroachment	750	12
Stormwater management	1,500	15
Sedimentation and soil erosion control	500	20
Sewer/treatment works	350	6
TOTAL	$6,650	

Source: Authors' calculations from survey document responses

Finally, we asked about the cost of application fees and other administrative requirements. Table 15 shows that approximately $13,000 can be added to a developer's per-unit costs in application, preparation, and review fees. (That figure does not include the cost of fair-share housing plans.) New Jersey is particularly costly because of the way development review is conducted. Developers pay to have plans drawn, then must place in escrow sufficient funds to cover a town's cost of reviewing those plans, often by contract engineers and attorneys. In North Carolina, by contrast, developers pay nominal fees, and a town's general tax revenue pays for review. As we show in the North Carolina case studies, however, there is pressure in several communities to increase developers' fees.

Procedural delays, the costs of which are incorporated in the responses summarized in tables 11 to 13, come from time lags in processing applications. As discussed in chapter 3, New Jersey's Municipal Land Use Law specifies a review period not to exceed ninety-five days for large projects. Yet, the median length of time required for typical subdivision reviews in New Jersey was twenty months, while zoning change petitions took fourteen months. Our surveys of builders/developers and regulators (state environmental officials and local planners and engineers), discussed in chapter 2, suggested that those delays result from a myriad of factors: a high number of requests for variances and waivers (for subdivision and

TABLE 14

Permit Review Times in New Jersey
—
New Jersey Department of Environmental Protection
Permit Activity Report: Land-Use Regulation Program

Permit Type	TOTAL AVERAGE REVIEW TIMES (Days)		
	July–December 1994	January–June 1995	July–December 1995
Waterfront development	76	80	79
Wetlands, Types A and B	70	58	80
Stream encroachment	45	46	52
Freshwater wetlands (general)	71	54	66
Freshwater wetlands (individual)	95	127	105
Freshwater wetlands: letter of interpretation	68	53	66
Freshwater wetlands: transition-area waiver	74	50	60
Freshwater wetlands: letter of exemption	141	58	58
Coastal Area Facility Review Act	66	52	63

Source: *Permit Activity Report.* Trenton, NJ: New Jersey Department of Environmental Protection (1994, 1995).

zoning changes); citizen opposition, especially among well-educated, higher-income residents of communities with home rule; too few and poorly trained staff members (for environmental permits); submission errors reflecting inadequate information to developers and lax screening; and overlapping jurisdictions, leading to the need for multiple reviews. Our surveys also suggested that these factors are not quite as prevalent in North Carolina communities as they are in New Jersey (Chapel Hill being an exception), and consequently, review periods in North Carolina are shorter.

Are twenty and fourteen months "too long"? In part, the answer depends on whom you ask. Builders/developers complain that municipalities often drag their heels intentionally; the subdivision review and zoning review processes, they say, should not take more than six and three months, respectively. Indeed, many claim to have used New Jersey Municipal Land Use Law and similar guidelines to form their expectations.

TABLE 15

New Jersey: Application and Compliance Cost Summary

	MEAN APPLICATION COST PER UNIT	n	MEAN DEVELOPERS' PREPARATION COST PER UNIT	n	MEAN COSTS ASSESSED BY LOCAL GOVERNMENT	n
Zoning/zoning change	$842	16	$1,936	17	$1,904	13
Subdivision plan review	$1,016	22	$1,076	20	$1,030	14
Environmental review	$291	17	$1,085	17	$1,180	9
Growth management	†		†		†	
Building inspection	†		$1,138	19	$1,611	13
Fair-share housing plan	$825	4	$4,000	2	$1,172	4
TOTAL: $19,106	$2,974		$9,235		$6,897	

Notes: Means and medians are similar because of data distribution.
† = No response

Source: Authors' calculations from survey document responses

Without conceding whether twenty and fourteen months are indeed too long, we can illustrate the impact of delays on a builder's bottom line. For a sample project comprising twenty-four units on lots costing an average of $20,000 each—the median characteristics of respondents' projects— we can calculate the carrying cost of an added twelve months of regulatory action. If we assume that a builder financed the $480,000 in land costs with an 80 percent loan at 7.5 percent, annual interest on the borrowed funds would be $28,800 ($1,200 for each of the twenty-four units). We can legitimately figure the carrying cost on the full $480,000, since there is an opportunity cost of not investing the 20 percent down payment amount at 7.5 percent. Thus the per-unit carrying cost would be $1,500 per year.

That additional $1,200 to $1,500 is almost equal to the per-unit difference in the price paid for improved versus raw land, as indicated in the builders/developers surveys. The median house in the survey responses was built on two-thirds of an acre, which cost $20,000 per lot on average. Respondents indicated that the median cost of site improvements was $22,000 per lot. They also indicated that the price paid for improved, approved lots was $43,329; $43,329 minus $22,000 minus $20,000 has a remainder of $1,329, which is what we estimated to be the approximate carrying cost of the land during the "delay" interval.

That illustration does not apply to all developers. Many of the respondents indicated that they were able to secure land options that were exercised only when approvals were received. Some of those options required a nonrefundable deposit; others did not. Even with that arrangement there is a carrying cost, because landowners tend to charge slightly more for land that is bought conditionally rather than outright. The premium charged varied greatly among the developers interviewed.

Due to the low response rate to our mail survey and its possible lack of representativeness, we conducted phone interviews with 66 builders/developers drawn from the same sample as our mail survey. We divided the interviewed parties into four panels. The first panel's respondents were asked the following questions:

> *Assuming that there is a demand in your market for completed homes selling for $500,000 on half-acre lots:*
>
> ☐ *In a typical case, what is the most you would spend on hard costs to build the house and appurtenances (brick, lumber, and direct labor)?*
>
> ☐ *In a typical situation, what is the most you would pay for the half-acre improved lot with all approvals in place (construction, subdivision, and environmental)? (Disregard the possibility of additional costs for impact fees, dedications, etc.)*
>
> ☐ *Again in a typical case, what is the most you would have paid for that same lot in a subdivision if approvals but no improvements were in place?*
>
> ☐ *What is the most you would have paid for that same lot in a subdivision with neither approvals nor improvements in place?*

We asked the same questions of the same panel of builders/developers regarding a $500,000 home on a two-acre lot.

Panel two was asked the same questions for half- and two-acre lots, but for a home selling for $250,000. Panel three was asked the questions for a $125,000 home on a half-acre lot, and panel four, for a $750,000 home on two acres.

These "willingness to pay" questions are consistent with the contingent valuation approach commonly used in environmental research (see Paterson, Luger, and Lindsay 1995). Our purpose in this case was to ascertain how builders value approvals and improvements. We used differently valued properties to account for possible nonlinearities in the demand curve. Table 16 reports the mean values.

TABLE 16

Home Sales Prices: Mean Values

Cost Category	One-Half Acre $	One-Half Acre n	Two Acres $	Two Acres n
Panel One: Home Sales Price = $500,000				
Hard costs	$273,077	13	$258,750	12
Improved, approved lot	134,615	13	140,357	14
Raw approved land	84,545	11	78,654	13
Raw unapproved land	51,696	14	56,125	14
Panel Two: Home Sales Price = $250,000				
Hard costs	$135,845	25	$139,026	19
Improved, approved lot	84,700	25	91,024	21
Raw approved land	46,888	20	55,515	17
Raw unapproved land	30,475	20	31,053	19
Panel Three: Home Sales Price = $125,000				
Hard costs	$76,024	21	—	
Improved, approved lot	34,643	21	—	
Raw approved land	21,235	17	—	
Raw unapproved land	17,434	19	—	
Panel Four: Home Sales Price = $750,000				
Hard costs	—		$404,417	6
Improved, approved lot	—		201,758	6
Raw approved land	—		94,583	6
Raw unapproved land	—		55,417	6

Source: Authors' calculations from survey document responses

The numbers in the table make sense. The half-acre lots are more expensive per acre than the two-acre parcels because they are in more-expensive locations. In other words, as we would expect, developers build more-expensive houses on smaller lots where land costs are higher. The brick-and-mortar costs of the houses should not differ by size of lot, unless there are differences in the cost of infrastructure (for example, building a well or septic tank as opposed to hooking up to a central system). The small differences seen between panels one and two are not statistically significant, using a t-test on the means.

Note that the price paid for improved, approved land plus the hard costs do not sum to the selling price. In part, that is a consequence of the data distribution (summing mean values). But there is also a profit margin to consider. The table indicates the following rates of return to builders/developers:

- ☐ For a $500,000 home on one-half acre: 22.6 percent
- ☐ For a $500,000 home on two acres: 25.3 percent
- ☐ For a $250,000 home on one-half acre: 13.4 percent
- ☐ For a $250,000 home on two acres: 8.9 percent
- ☐ For a $125,000 home on one-half acre: 13.0 percent
- ☐ For a $750,000 home on two acres: 23.7 percent

Those estimates are consistent with what builders/developers claim in interviews: that higher rates of return accrue to higher-valued property, perhaps because the price elasticity of demand for housing is relatively small for the highest-income households, allowing more regulatory costs to be passed forward. Note that the figures are rough proxies of actual rates of return, because they do not include financing costs and are not annualized. Clearly, the longer a development project takes, the lower the annualized rate of return, which is the relevant indicator of financial viability.

The data in table 16 generally reflect our mail survey responses from New Jersey builders/developers. The median price of new homes built by our respondents was $236,000. The median size of a developed lot was 0.8 acres. The cost of the raw land component of that parcel was $24,000, and the median cost for improvements per parcel was $27,900.

The responses in table 16 can be translated into the costs for lots that are approved/unimproved as well as for lots that are improved/approved, as shown in table 17.

TABLE 17

Cost of Approvals and Improvements †

Difference between Land That Is:	Lot Size	
	ONE-HALF ACRE	TWO ACRES
Home Sales Price = $500,000		
Improved/approved and unimproved/approved	$55,000	$60,193
Improved/approved and unimproved/unapproved	80,480	84,233
Unimproved/approved and unimproved/unapproved	27,187	25,903
Home Sales Price = $250,000		
Improved/approved and unimproved/approved	$42,511	$44,630
Improved/approved and unimproved/unapproved	53,833	60,068
Unimproved/approved and unimproved/unapproved	16,381	18,035
Home Sales Price = $125,000		
Improved/approved and unimproved/approved	$21,559	—
Improved/approved and unimproved/unapproved	22,014	—
Unimproved/approved and unimproved/unapproved	1,983	—
Home Sales Price = $750,000		
Improved/approved and unimproved/approved		$128,610
Improved/approved and unimproved/unapproved	—	175,610
Unimproved/approved and unimproved/unapproved	—	39,167

Note: † = These are *mean differences,* **not** *differences in mean values* as shown in table 16.

Source: Authors' calculations from survey document responses

These are hypothetical offer prices. For example, a developer would be willing to pay $27,187 more for unimproved land with approvals than for unimproved land without approvals for a planned $500,000 home on half an acre. As we would expect, the more expensive a home, the larger the difference. Note that the relatively small differences between the mean values for one-half acre and two-acre lots were not significant as measured by a t-test. The first row in each panel of the table also provides a basis for estimating the cost of improvements. That number ranges from 10.7 percent to 15.1 percent of the sales price. It is worth noting that the hypothetical cost of improvements, if weighted by the mix of differently valued homes in New Jersey, would be in the $22,000 range, as was revealed in the written developer surveys. The survey responses indicated that per-lot improvements cost 11.8 percent of the sales price.

Table 17 is based on the assumption that developers have target markets in mind when undertaking projects and that changes in the cost of approvals affect the pricing of land. Of course, that is an extreme assumption. Consider, for example, a $125,000 house on a half-acre lot. A landowner may agree to sell that lot without approvals or improvements for $20,000, not $17,434. A developer would then assess whether the extra $2,600 could be passed on to a buyer, or if he or she could live with a lower rate of return. The answer depends on market conditions in a particular place at a particular moment in time (as reflected in the price elasticity of demand).

The issue of the incidence of cost changes for structures and land was addressed empirically by C. T. Somerville (1996). He demonstrates that unexpected changes in the cost of land—due, for example, to unanticipated regulatory delays—are borne in the short run by builders or developers in lower profits, but unexpected increases in the cost of a structure can be passed on to consumers in higher final prices. Therefore, "builder behavior" would be expected to be much more sensitive to land costs because they directly affect the builder's bottom line" (p. 140). In the longer run, diminished supply would affect prices through normal supply-and-demand adjustments.

That empirical finding is important. It affects our interpretation of a supply-side model as presented in standard texts. See, for example, Maisel and Roulac (1976) and Mills (1972).

Consider equation 1:

$$H = \Lambda S^\alpha L^\beta \tag{1}$$

where H is the output of housing, measured as a bundle that includes land and buildings; S and L represent structures and land, respectively; and Λ, α, and β are parameters that represent neutral technical progress and the shares of structures and land in production, respectively. Assuming constant or only slightly increasing economies of scale, α and β will each be less than unity.

Differentiating (1) with respect to land ($\partial H / \partial L$) and setting that equal to the real "rental rate" on land (r), as would be appropriate in long-run equilibrium, yields the expression shown in equation 2:

$$pH = \frac{rL}{\beta} \qquad (2)$$

Here, pH is the cost of housing and rL is the cost of the land required for its production. A dollar change in land costs (the numerator on the right-hand side), due, for example, to regulation, changes housing costs (the left-hand side) by more than a dollar, as long as β is less than one. For example, for a parameter value of 0.5, a dollar increase in land costs (rL) would have to be accompanied by a two-dollar increase in housing costs (pH) for equality to prevail.

The smaller β is (less than one), the larger the change in housing costs for any dollar change in land costs. Since β is directly proportional to the elasticity of demand for housing with respect to the price of land, we can see that less-elastic demand allows regulatory costs to be passed forward more readily. Because land is immobile, there should be a lower own-price elasticity of demand for it than for structures; that was also theorized by Somerville (1996).

That theoretical fact explains what is commonly referred to as the builder's "rule of thumb:" a 2:1 to 4:1 relationship between land and selling costs. That ratio is illustrated in table 16 (between the price of approved, improved land and the selling price) and by equations (1) and (2). Note that the rule-of-thumb multiplier depends on how a builder/developer allocates costs. If improvements are included as part of hard costs, the ratio of selling price-to-land costs is higher than the ratio of selling price-to-approved and improved land. We are not aware of any convention in the literature regarding how to calculate the multiplier.

The rule-of-thumb multiplier was evident in our analysis of mail surveys from New Jersey builders/developers. For example, eight respondents estimated the median increase in the price of a house due to zoning restrictions (which required them to change the design and/or layout of their projects) to be $50,000. Using the multiplier of 4.0 for the ratio between sales price changes and raw land price value, that should translate backward into a raw land price difference of $12,500. Indeed, the respondents who provided an estimate of the change in raw land value due to zoning restrictions gave a median figure of approximately $7,000. The higher implied multiplier (close to 7.0) may well be an artifact of the small and unrepresentative sample of builders/developers responding to that question; however, it is of the right order of magnitude.

This evidence is significant because it demonstrates that there is more than a dollar-for-dollar relationship between regulatory costs and final housing prices. The extent of the cost translation will vary from project to project depending on local conditions, the size of the house, land-to-structures ratio, and other factors. The translation occurs to some degree whether the cost of regulation is accounted for in the nonland (structures) or land component of the housing bundle since both share parameters, α and β, are less than unity. However, the impact is greater for those elements of land costs since $\beta \leq \alpha$.

The relationship between regulation and housing costs helps us understand some of the survey responses. Builders/developers indicated, for example, that open space set-asides caused them to raise the price of a median finished unit by $3,500. Using a multiplier of 4.0, that means that the actual outlay for additional land was about $900 per unit. Similarly, delay costs tend to be translated into higher sales prices with that multiplier effect. For example, we noted earlier that each 12-month delay adds approximately $1,500 per unit in additional carrying costs, which would translate into $6,000 more for a buyer, at most. (That translates into 2.54 percent of the median housing price per year, or 0.2 percent per month. That is less than the 1.2 percent per month estimated by Seidel [1978]; our lower figure presumably reflects changes in interest rates and housing values since that time.) Builders, however, react in various short-term ways to regulatory costs. In the next chapter we discuss evidence that suggests how markets adjust to unexpected regulatory costs.

SURVEY RESPONSES ABOUT INCIDENCE

The surveys suggest that not all compliance costs associated with government regulations are immediately passed along in the form of higher housing prices. Some developers, constrained from offering housing, are forced to accept a lower rate of return. Thirty percent of respondents (67 of 230) indicated, for example, that they accepted lower profits as a result of environmental requirements. On average, environmental requirements reduced the rate of return by 2.4 percentage points (and 1 percentage point as a median) for the six who answered that question.

However, the major reason cited for not developing in areas with complex local regulations was that it was too bothersome. The "hassle factor" is often the reason developers choose not to build in particular areas. As mentioned earlier, developers believe the approval process is too lengthy

TABLE 18

Incidence of Regulatory Costs in New Jersey

Regulation Type	Number of Responses	Number of Respondents Indicating They Reduced Price Offered for Land	Number of Respondents Indicating Price of Units Was Increased	Median Change in Selling Price	
					(n)
Subdivision	57	19	19	$20,000/unit	13
Zoning	64	22	10	$50,000/unit	8
Environmental	230	74	39	$11,750	6

Source: Authors' calculations from survey document responses

and that the review periods allowed governments are three to four times longer than necessary. That is particularly true with environmental regulations, where most projects need the approval of more than one jurisdiction. Not only does this add to the time necessary to secure approvals, but often two different jurisdictions have inconsistent requirements. That leads to time-consuming negotiations among the parties.

The "hassle factor" also was addressed by Rosen and Katz (1981, 33) in their study of 700 single-family dwellings in the San Francisco area:

> Developers . . . cope with a complex regulatory environment by either not building in areas with restrictive regulations, or proposing subdivisions that go beyond even the most restrictive subdivision regulations.

Table 18 summarizes the survey responses regarding the incidence of subdivision and zoning requirements. The main point illustrated by the table is that regulations can impact on more than one level. Some developers respond by lowering their bid for land, thereby impacting the landowner, whereas others shift the burden forward in the form of higher housing prices. The response varies by developer, by market, by time, and by type of regulation. In the short run, it is unusual for costs to be fully shifted forward to home buyers. That throws into doubt the many studies that assume that all regulatory costs are borne by the home-buying public.

STATISTICAL ANALYSIS

In addition to the findings presented in this chapter, we assessed the relationship between restrictions and development outcomes with a statistical model that specifies development outcomes as a function of possible explanatory variables, including the stringency of the types of regulations.

Because we were interested in the effect of differences in local ordinances and the implementation by local governments of state and federal regulations pertaining to residential development, we used the municipality as the unit of analysis.

Our next task was to define an appropriate dependent variable. We chose the number of housing units authorized by building permits issued per year in each municipality, largely because of the availability of those data. If the law of supply and demand operates, then the volume of authorized new housing units should be correlated with changes in housing prices, with higher prices characterizing slow-growth areas if all else is equal. We averaged the number of authorized new housing units for three years (1990–1992) to smooth out fluctuations.

Using the literature as a guide, we defined the basic model as follows:

$$P = \alpha + \beta X + \varepsilon \qquad (3)$$

at time t, where P is a vector of n-dependent variable values, α is an estimated constant, β is a vector of m-estimated coefficients, X is an $m \times n$ matrix of explanatory variables, and ε is an error term assumed to be normally distributed with a mean of 0 and standard deviation of σ. This is a standard multiple regression model assumed to satisfy the necessary econometric conditions.

Table 19 contains a list of the explanatory variables used in the estimation (i.e., $X_1, X_2 ... X_m$ in equation [3]). It also indicates the direction of effect we expect.

The inclusion of regional dummies (NY and PHL) allows us to test the hypothesis that the areas in highest demand—those within commuting distance of New York City and Philadelphia—will have housing markets different from those of the rest of the state. We indicate an expected positive effect for these variables due to the demand pressures in those markets. These dummies are important as controls even if no causal relationship is hypothesized.

Stable is included to test the relationship between previous in-migration and new building activity. On the one hand, it could be argued that

TABLE 19

Variables Expected to Account for Differences in Authorized New Housing Units

Variable Abbreviation	Variable Description	Expected Sign
NY	Dummy variable = 1 if county is within the New York City MSA	+
PHL	Dummy variable = 1 if county is within the Philadelphia MSA	+
Stable	Percentage of municipality residents over 16 who resided in the county between 1985 and 1990	?
S-FRatio	Mean student–faculty ratio during 1993 in primary schools within the municipality's school district	+
Services	Municipality's total per-household budget for fire, police, and garbage service, 1990	?
PropTax	Equalized property tax rate for the municipality, 1990	?
Income	Median household income in municipality, 1990	−
VacLand	Vacant acres within the municipality in 1990, multiplied by the percentage of assessed property zoned residential	+
Restrict	Dummy variable = 1 if municipality is within the high restrictive category based on survey of local regulators to questions regarding the development process in the municipality	−

municipalities comprised of new entrants would be most welcoming and would have active developers interested in building more. On the other hand, the sign could be negative if the recent migrants wanted to "bar the door."

The *S-FRatio* variable captures the effect of school quality on an area's residential desirability. The higher the value, the more building activity we expect, all else being equal.

Services is included to account for noneducational spending. We are unsure about the expected sign because fire and police expenditures can reflect either a higher level of public safety or a need to deal with a high level of public safety problems. The inclusion of that variable makes the *S-FRatio* variable more meaningful, since it controls for the possibility that school spending occurs at the expense of other common municipal services.

PropTax is another control, since the Tiebout argument is that people choose the most preferred service-tax combination. High property taxes should dampen demand and be associated with less development.

Income is included to account for the presence of exclusionary practices by higher-income communities. We expect high-income enclaves to make development difficult, not only through restrictive practices but because large-lot zoning and similar fiscal requirements put housing out of the reach of most homebuyers.

VacLand is included to capture the supply-side pressure to develop. The higher that value, the more we expect developers to seek development permission.

Finally, *Restrict* is our measure of regulatory stringency in a municipality, as per interviews with municipal planners and engineers. Respondents were asked three indicator questions by phone:

- ☐ Based on your general knowledge of (municipality name), what percentage of subdivision applications are approved within 95 days of their submission to the town?

- ☐ How would you characterize the attitudes of residents in the municipality toward new development of residential housing?

- ☐ Given the town's location, history, and other external factors, and combining subdivision, zoning change, and environmental regulations, how do you think developers perceive your community in terms of developing new housing?

The three sets of responses were scaled into an index that ranged from 5 to 13, with lower values indicating greater restrictiveness. Table 20 lists 70 townships in order of their restrictiveness index and group (high, low). We created a dummy variable that took the value of 1 for all municipalities classified in the high group. Twenty-six observations were discarded because of suspect data (e.g., inconsistent responses).

The ranking of townships is interesting in its own right. Our concern, however, is to relate the ranking (and other variables) to differences among townships in building permit activity, controlling for other variables. That is done using equation 3. The results are reported in table 21.

TABLE 20

Restrictiveness Scores

County	Township	Group	Index
BURLINGTON	Hainesport Township	High	5
PASSAIC	Ringwood Township	High	5
HUNTERDON	Alexandria Township	High	6
MONMOUTH	Middletown Township	High	6
SOMERSET	Montgomery Township	High	6
SUSSEX	Sparta Township	High	6
ESSEX	West Orange Township	High	7
MIDDLESEX	Woodbridge Township	High	7
MONMOUTH	Howell Township	High	7
MORRIS	Randolph Township	High	7
SOMERSET	Hillsborough Township	High	7
WARREN	Allamuchy Township	High	7
BERGEN	Teaneck Township	High	8
BERGEN	Wyckoff Township	High	8
GLOUCESTER	Franklin Township	High	8
HUDSON	North Bergen Township	High	8
HUNTERDON	Lebanon Township	High	8
SALEM	Elsinboro	High	8
SALEM	Mannington	High	8
SALEM	Pennsville	High	8
SALEM	Pittsgrove	High	8
SALEM	Quinton	High	8
SALEM	Salem City	High	8
SALEM	Upper Pittsgrove	High	8
SOMERSET	Bedminster Township	High	8
SUSSEX	Vernon Township	High	8
BERGEN	Ramsey Borough	High	9
ESSEX	Belleville Township	High	9
ESSEX	Bloomfield Township	High	9
HUNTERDON	Holland Township	High	9
MIDDLESEX	Cranbury	High	9
MIDDLESEX	Monroe Township	High	9
MONMOUTH	Spring Lake	High	9

TABLE 20 (CONTINUED)

County	Township	Group	Index
MORRIS	Denville Township	High	9
SALEM	Alloway Township	High	9
SUSSEX	Byram Township	High	9
HUNTERDON	Califon Boro	High	9
WARREN	Hackettstown	High	9
BERGEN	Emerson Borough	High	10
BERGEN	Ridgewood Village	High	10
BURLINGTON	Pemberton Township	High	10
MIDDLESEX	South Plainfield Borough	High	10
MONMOUTH	Asbury Park	High	10
MONMOUTH	Belmar Borough	High	10
MONMOUTH	Farmingdale	High	10
MONMOUTH	Spring Lake Heights	High	10
PASSAIC	Clifton City	High	10
WARREN	Belvidere	High	10
ATLANTIC	Hamilton Township	Low	11
CUMBERLAND	City of Bridgeton	Low	11
CUMBERLAND	Deerfield Township	Low	11
CUMBERLAND	Downe Township	Low	11
CUMBERLAND	Lawrence Township	Low	11
ESSEX	West Caldwell Township	Low	11
HUNTERDON	Franklin Township	Low	11
MERCER	Ewing Township	Low	11
MIDDLESEX	New Brunswick	Low	11
OCEAN	Seaside Heights	Low	11
SOMERSET	Bernards Township	Low	11
SUSSEX	Ogdensburg Borough	Low	11
UNION	Linden City	Low	11
CAMDEN	Bellmawr Borough	Low	12
ESSEX	Newark City	Low	12
HUDSON	Bayonne City	Low	12
PASSAIC	Paterson City	Low	12
SUSSEX	Hopatcong Borough	Low	12
UNION	Cranford Township	Low	12
HUNTERDON	Readington Township	Low	13
WARREN	White Township	Low	13

Source: Constructed by authors from telephone interview data provided by municipal planners and engineers. See Appendix II.

TABLE 21

Regression Results

Variable Name	Parameter Estimate	Standard Error	T for H_0: Parameter = 0	Prob. > /T/
NY	-5.640446	7.6225982	-0.74	0.4622
PHL	1.065741	14.934951	0.071	0.9433
Stable	-48.16702	38.410859	-1.254	0.2147
S-FRatio	1.365081	1.2156699	1.123	0.266
Services	0.005915	0.0114759	0.515	0.6082
Income	0.000228	0.0002661	0.858	0.3942
PropTax	1.748241	7.2101125	0.242	0.8092
VacLand	0.001473	0.0004325	3.406	0.0012
Restrict	-12.14181	6.4984663	-1.868	0.0666

Notes: N = 70
R^2 = 0.365
Adjusted R^2 = 0.269
Model F Value = 3.826, Prob. > F = 0.0007

Source: Authors' calculations

The most important result shown in table 21 is in the last row. The negative sign confirms that the towns in New Jersey that perceived themselves (and, presumably, that were perceived by others) to have a more restrictive development process tended to have fewer authorized housing units in the early 1990s. That statistical result corroborates the survey evidence, at least on the "hassle factor."[24]

We cannot infer that less building activity due to a perception of greater restrictiveness means higher or lower land prices. If developable land were available in restrictive communities, the restrictions should put downward pressure on land prices. But the restrictions themselves may require developers to pay more per parcel—for example, if there are minimum parcel sizes.

The validity of the model is confirmed by the performance of the other variables. The coefficients on all but VacLand are, most likely, not different from zero. Those that have a probability value (for differing from zero) of less than 0.30 have signs that are not contrary to expectations. The negative sign on *Stable* suggests that the more migration there has been into a municipality in the past several years, the less building there is likely to be. We referred to that as the "bar the door" syndrome. In the case of New Jersey, where developable land is often at a premium, the appropriate adage might be "no more room at the inn." The school quality variable (*S-FRatio*) also has the expected sign. The other highly significant variable is on vacant land, which is shown to be positively related to authorized new housing units.

6

Community Case Studies in New Jersey and North Carolina

We conducted four case studies in New Jersey (Princeton Borough and Township, Mendham Township, Middletown, and Mount Laurel) and five in North Carolina (Chapel Hill, Cary, Jacksonville, Durham, and Concord). For each case study, we interviewed at least two developers working in the jurisdiction, as well as several senior appointed and/or elected officials (for example, planners, engineers, mayors). We also interviewed several developers of lower-income or entry-level housing in different locations in each state in order to assess the specific impact of regulation on the low end of the market.[25]

It was not our objective in choosing two states in which to conduct case studies to achieve generalizability. Our primary focus is on New Jersey, since that state was believed to have particularly burdensome regulations. We use North Carolina as a benchmark or touchstone in order to judge the New Jersey experience against at least one different place. We could have used any number of states similarly. However, we knew from having done other projects in North Carolina that that state was less bureaucratic and generally more development friendly. Choosing North Carolina also enabled us to minimize fieldwork costs, since it is our home base.

We include the complete case study reports in order to show the complexity and richness of the issue of regulation and housing affordability at the community level. Different communities face different pressures from

87

community groups and residents, consequently using and responding to regulations differently.

NEW JERSEY CASE STUDIES

In all of the New Jersey communities where we conducted case studies, housing prices are high. For example, a Princeton developer discussed a project that consisted of town houses selling in the $400,000 to $500,000 range. A project in Middletown consisted of 27 units with a minimum price per home of $280,000. The cost of housing in Mendham is no less expensive; here, improved five-acre lots usually sell for between $185,000 and $227,500. Mount Laurel provided the widest range of housing prices in our sample.

New Jersey's high housing prices are partially due to high land costs that result from the relative scarcity of buildable land in the state. For example, Mendham Township's population in 1990 was approximately 4,600. The master plan developed by the local planning department estimated that the maximum population when "buildout" occurred would be 6,000. In fact, only 9 percent of the land in Mendham is available for new development. Thus, the high cost of new housing is caused in part by structural characteristics of the real estate market. However, certain procedural aspects of the development process add costs, and it is those procedural complexities that cause the greatest amount of frustration for developers.

Each of the New Jersey sites required that a new development be approved by a planning board. There are differences, however, with respect to the level of detail required in plans submitted for approval. For example, because builders in Middletown must present fully engineered plans to the planning board, most ask for an informal review of their plans before they submit them. That informal review is especially critical for projects that include a deviation from the town's master plan.

The process is slightly different in Princeton Borough and Township. Concept plans, which do not include formal measurements but generally are consistent with existing zoning and master plan requirements, are submitted for review and discussion by the planning board. Those plans are reviewed by a planner, an engineer, and a zoning officer to weed out proposals deemed objectionable to residents. A concept plan that makes it through the review is presented by the planning board in a forum where the public, the town staff, and the developer can exchange ideas about the project. Since planning board decisions usually are consistent with feedback received at the concept plan level, the public can help shape a proposed development. That last issue is particularly important to local residents, who can be instrumental in slowing unwanted development.

In Mendham, a technical review committee must approve fully engineered development plans before the local planning board will act upon them. That committee also encourages developers to submit concept plans so that it can ensure that those plans conform to mandated technical requirements.

As is true elsewhere in New Jersey, the planning boards in all the case study communities decide whether to approve a proposed development. All the developers we interviewed thought that planning board decisions were based on a plan's technical merits, not on residents' political sentiments. That is not to say that planning boards do not consider public opinion. According to a town engineer, planning board decisions are "hard to generalize . . . they are really made on a case-by-case basis. Some decisions are more political than others; some are entirely professional." A developer said, "Public input is the biggest factor in slowing down the process. . . . Sometimes projects are rejected for political interests, but it doesn't happen frequently."

Most of the developers interviewed believed that planning board reviews were not a major factor in delaying projects. Town master plans usually have been developed with significant public input. Therefore, according to one developer, "[I]f you go in with plans consistent with the master plan you will get approval the majority of the time." Most developers agreed that the planning board review process was thorough, but not ridiculously so. Nonetheless, planning boards do not always make decisions within the ninety-five days mandated for large projects. Planning board approval for one project took seven months; the plans had to be redrawn ten times because of variance and subdivision waivers. Sometimes delay is due to the complexity of a project. If a planning board asks a developer for an extension because it needs to study a project in greater detail, most developers, according to our interviews, feel they must grant it. If they don't, the project is likely to be rejected out of hand.

Developers describe extralegal regulations, not local planning boards, as the major source of delay in New Jersey. The rules of the New Jersey Department of Environmental Protection were cited most often. One developer mentioned a water quality management plan that required almost ten months for approval because of DEP staffing problems—and getting it done in that length of time took a fair amount of political clout and a great deal of attention to detail.

According to one developer, DEP can delay even a project already approved by the Army Corps of Engineers. In one such case, DEP required a developer in compliance with federal guidelines on wetlands mitigation to complete an historical and cultural survey. Even though the wetlands in question comprised only a quarter-acre of the parcel, DEP believed the survey was required under the Freshwater Wetlands Protection Act and because the tract had structures from a previous use. In addition, a citizens group attempted to reverse the developer's appeals, basing its opposition on ambiguous understandings of wetlands and other environmental regulation.

Regardless of the source of delay, bringing new housing to market in New Jersey takes time. One project that received preliminary approvals in 1987 still had no units built by 1996. Another project started in 1987 was not completed until 1994 because of changes to stormwater management requirements. A project in Princeton was delayed because the developer disputed the tax assessor's valuation of the purchased finished lots. All those delays add to the costs of developing housing while increasing the risks associated with a new project.

Costs of Delay in the Approval Process

Such costs are not trivial. A developer we interviewed estimated that the cost associated with delays in one project was $11,390 per unit, 3 percent of the final selling price of the houses in the development. A major component of that cost was the salary and overhead paid to the developer's staff to change the assessor's valuation of the improved lots. That project in Middletown, delayed by changes in the Freshwater Wetlands Protection Act, incurred costs of $1 million. Another developer estimated the cost of securing approvals for a five-lot project at $67,000, $47,000 of which was spent on redrawing plans he felt were adequate at the time of submission.

In the above-cited cases, the costs associated with bureaucratic delay were passed forward in the form of higher home prices. However, another developer described a project where costs associated with delay were borne by a landowner, not by a home buyer. In that case, a landowner's property was rezoned from agricultural to residential use before the deal was closed. Therefore, the owner paid higher property taxes for fourteen months before receiving the proceeds from the sale. In addition, the purchaser of the land offered $300,000 less for the property because of higher overhead expenses associated with delays in bringing the units to market. According to the developer, higher costs are not always passed forward to the consumer: "Ultimately, the market determines the selling price for a house, not the builder."

 **NEW JERSEY CASE STUDY**

Princeton Borough and Princeton Township

Princeton Borough in Mercer County, the home of Princeton University, is a small, upscale town with a very defined commercial area. The borough is only 1.9 square miles in area; in 1990 it had a median family income of $60,927. The borough's 1990 population was 12,016, 44 percent of which were college students. Princeton Township, which is also upscale, is a less-dense growing suburban area surrounding the borough. We looked at these two communities in tandem because the two governments have a combined planning board of representatives from each, with planning board members voting on applications regardless of host jurisdiction.

We interviewed the township's engineer and three executives from a local development company: its president, vice president, and estimator.

The Engineer

According to the engineer, "Generally, Princeton residents are very well educated and quite savvy—they know what they can do and what they cannot do." They tend, he said, not to come out against projects they know they have no right to alter. He went on to say that "residents understand the zoning process is a more logical arena in which to influence the development of the town, and they are involved in that process." In fact, he said,

> Zoning was set up to create the development expected to generate the demographic change that will meet the expected capacities of the township. The same thing goes for traffic flows, etc.
>
> We ran a simulation of the township at full buildout to see where there would be traffic problems, to check the expected demographic changes, and so on. We adjusted the planning process from the findings of this simulation study.

That master planning process, he said, "had lots of public participation; lots of people came out and were involved." As a result, the highest number ever to oppose a project was seventy-five, unlike other places where hundreds may protest development.

On a scale of 1 (technical) to 5 (political), the engineer rates the planning board decision process as a 1. But he also said, "Public involvement is very important to the planning board. It is willing to make minor suggestions and alterations to plans to suit the public."

In Princeton, full engineering drawings are not required for application reviews, but developers are encouraged to present concept plans, with notification to neighbors and the planning board. About that process, the engineer stated:

> They [the members of the planning board] find it is easier to work with applicants at the concept plan level: changes are easier to make; it's very difficult to make/implement suggestions once engineered drawings are involved.

> The decision on a concept plan is not formally voted on by the planning board— it is purely an exchange of ideas. But there are reports filed by the township's professionals about a project at the conceptual level.

> They [the members of the planning board] feel that public opposition to projects is much less when the public is able to make its feelings known at the conceptual level, where there is a chance to influence the project.

The engineer explained why the planning board does not vote at the concept plan level.

> The concept plan does not include formal measurements/surveys/delineations, etc. The board would need to know these, to know the lot yield, the lot layout, environmental constraints, etc. It is impossible to vote on a project without knowing these things, and these things cannot be known until the project is crystallized into engineered drawings.

But he also said that planning board decisions are generally consistent with feedback provided at the concept plan level—that "the board tries hard to send one message."

Thus, he says, few projects are even proposed that are inconsistent with existing zoning, and "those would be weeded out at the concept plan level." He said they use a team approach in reviewing plans—the planner, engineer, and zoning officer all sit down together.

Regarding multiple-jurisdiction problems, the engineer said they used to have difficulty with stormwater regulations: There are local, county, and Delaware and Raritan Canal Commission regulations. But they worked it out with the county and the Canal Commission so that those two jurisdictions accept Princeton's review.

The township engineer thought the state permitting process should rely more on an applicant's professional consultants to help with the review process.

The reviews for stream encroachment and wetlands should be improved. There is a thirty-day review program for minor stream encroachment issues. But the state should use developer professionals to do floodplain and wetlands delineations. They could be subject to spot-checking by DEP.

Having developers utilize good engineers and making them responsible for many of the review items would greatly simplify the permitting process.

He did note that substandard engineering is rarely a problem in Princeton.

The Developers

In 1993 the development company bought thirty-four lots from a bank for a fixed cost per lot, plus interest and taxes. Some improvements on the lots had already been made, and the company agreed to take care of the remainder. The bank, in turn, agreed to supply the necessary capital for those improvements. Although the bank was owed $4 million on the land, the total outlay for the project, including all site improvements, was $1,600,000.

Because the company had not been involved in the approval phase of the project, we focused on how regulation impacted the construction phase.[26]

When we conducted our interviews in August 1996, the company was following the original builder's concept by building town houses selling in the $400,000 to $500,000 range. At the time of the interview, the value of a finished lot was about $100,000 and the cost to build a 3,400-square-foot town house (sticks, bricks, labor, no land) was about $272,000.

The developers claimed they incurred excess regulatory costs. They based that belief on their experience; they have built many projects in New Jersey and Florida. They had three primary complaints about the town engineer's office:

1. *Excessive delays in getting construction permits*, which they estimated took about three weeks longer than what was reasonable.

   Assuming a marginal cost of capital equal to 15 percent, excluding overhead and management costs, the cost of that delay is simply the cost of holding the lot in question another three weeks, or

   $$3/52 * .15 * \$100,000 = \$865$$

2. *Excessive delays in inspections* because the town engineer's office strictly enforced a seventy-two-hour notice requirement for inspections.

That cost was impossible for the builders to break out and quantify, but it is a part of their perceived excess management costs, discussed below.

3. *Excessive delays in getting certificates of occupancy*: The developers estimated that it took two weeks to obtain each certificate.

Again assuming a marginal cost of capital equal to 15 percent, excluding overhead and management costs, the cost of this delay is simply the cost of holding the completed home another two weeks, at the selling price less broker's commission of 5 percent, or

$$2/52 * .15 * .95 * \$400,000 = \$2,192$$

The developers we interviewed also thought that the tax assessor was a significant source of regulatory cost; they accused her of simply trying to raise more money for the government. She first assessed each lot at $115,000, taking the position that it was worth one-quarter of the selling price of the finished house. On the other hand, the developers thought they had bought the lots at fair market value—otherwise the bank would have sold them for more—and that the assessment should reflect their purchase price. The tax assessor's outside consultant agreed with the developers, but a debate with the tax assessor's office ensued nonetheless. She first called to "make a deal," then to give them "my final offer." Eventually, however, the first four lots were assessed at $115,000 and the remainder at $65,000. Although the developers argued that even $65,000 was too high an assessment and attributed that cost to excessive regulation, we do not necessarily agree. We merely point out that there may be a cost.

Finally, the developers believed that it was due only to excruciating attention to the bureaucratic process and "reminding" regulators on a daily basis that they were awaiting permits or inspections or reviews that the project was built at all. They estimated that the excessive time spent on such attention to detail amounted to one-half of a superintendent, or $50,000 per year.[27] They were selling approximately eight homes a year, so that cost was $8,333.

In total, then, the developers calculated that their cost due to excessive regulation during the construction phase alone was:

+ (Costs of delays by town engineer's office) + (Cost of excess management to minimize delays)

= ($865 + $2,192) + ($8,333) = $11,390 per unit

That figure amounts to approximately 3 percent of the selling price.

 **NEW JERSEY CASE STUDY**

Mendham Township

Mendham Township is an eighteen-square-mile community in Morris County, New Jersey. The 1995 population was about 4,600; at total buildout, the master plan estimates a population of 6,000. In 1990 the median family income in Mendham was $107,288. The township's character is almost entirely residential, and many homes are on large lots. There is a small amount of commercial property and no industry; about 9 percent of the land is vacant or farmland.

We interviewed a long-time member of the Mendham planning board who at one time was mayor; the planning board's attorney; and two builders/developers.

The Planning Board

When the Planning Board member's tenure began in 1983, the board was developing a master plan that would allow cluster and/or town house development. The township's citizens had always been opposed to cluster development, but Mendham was one of the first communities in New Jersey to be taken to court under *Mount Laurel II.* Three large pieces of property were rezoned and approved to accommodate the township's full share of *Mount Laurel* housing: one tract of fourteen units and two tracts of twelve units each. The board member and the attorney agree that the state planning process, and *Mount Laurel* in particular, have not affected Mendham Township: Rezoning in the 1980s addressed the issue of affordable housing.

The planning board has used the same professional consultants for years: The planner had been there for more than twenty-five years; the engineer for more than fifteen; and the attorney we interviewed for nearly thirty years. After environmental regulations became more complex, the planning board also began to employ a professional environmental consulting firm; that firm had worked for the township for eight years.

Those professionals charge hourly fees for services and to attend meetings. During a meeting with multiple projects, only the time spent on a specific project is billed to the project. The planning board's attorney bills

$115 per hour for meetings, as well as for time other than meetings he spends on planning projects; this is less than half his fee for private clients. Some applicants question the fees of the professionals, wondering in particular whether such charges are really necessary, especially when a project is not in an environmentally sensitive area.

At the time the case study was conducted, the planning board was all Republican. The member we interviewed indicated that while the township is "solidly Republican," there have been Democrats appointed to the board. According to her, the ethics law enacted in the early 1990s had great impact on the planning board. Members and potential members alike resented the fact that they had to file financial disclosures as well as reveal real estate holdings. While they agreed with the need to eliminate conflicts of interest, they thought the law was intrusive.

The Application Process

The planning board has a technical review committee (TRC) made up of three planning board members, all technical personnel, and one representative each from the environmental commission and the township's historic committee. The TRC meets monthly to make sure applications are in technical compliance and to deem them complete. If, however, an applicant requests waivers from a planning board requirement, he or she must also appear before the full planning board.

Applicants usually bring concept plans to the TRC, especially if they are seeking to change existing rules (e.g., zoning). That preliminary step saves engineering costs. However, fully engineered plans are ultimately required. As one of the developers pointed out, "The TRC is mandatory and very complete; when it requires changes you have to redraw the plans." There is a checklist that must be met in submitted plans, but the checklist is not up to date. "Frequently, they will require things that are not on the checklist, claiming that they are to be added," the developer asserted.

The attorney said that on a scale of 1 to 5, where 1 is technical and 5 is political, he would rate the planning board decision process as a 2. He thinks the planning board relies heavily on the staff's technical reviews but that it gives more than lip service to the public. He says that if the public's concerns are legitimate, the board tries to craft approvals that address them. The planning board member we interviewed declined to rank the planning board's decision process: She didn't like the term "political." She prefers to describe the process as "listening to people who live in a community and pay taxes."

The attorney asserted that Mendham Township is an easy place in which to build because there is very little opposition to development; everyone just wants it done the right way. Both the builders to whom we spoke agreed. They thought the process was thorough but not onerous. They did, however, believe the process added significantly to their costs.

One of the developers said that the board assumes a "give us an extension or we'll deny you" attitude when it is taking longer than the allowed time to reach a decision. The attorney believes that the legislated time frame is unrealistic. "There are too many issues to consider. In towns like Mendham, all the easy developments are gone." He added that most problems originate with an applicant's professionals: "They don't meet deadlines, or they submit incomplete work. Problems generally aren't from the planning board or its staff."

The planning board member agreed that most applications in Mendham Township are not acted on in ninety days, especially when large projects are involved. She also agreed that the delay is most often due to project experts not submitting documents in required form. In her view, the board requests extensions most often because it has not received necessary information from a developer.

Both the planning board member and the attorney felt strongly that the New Jersey Builders Association's initiative to turn planning boards into policymakers and to delegate project review and approvals to professionals was ill-founded. The planning board member called the proposal an "obnoxious, corruption-prone idea" and believed that home rule should and will remain in force.

Developer I

This developer owns a business his father established in 1933. He was born and raised and still lives in Mendham. He is chairman of the township's historic preservation committee and is friendly with everyone on the planning board.[28]

Three of his sons work with him in the company, which builds custom homes and does some rehabilitation and restoration work. We talked with him about a twelve-lot subdivision he had recently put through preliminary, road, construction, and final approval. Of those twelve lots, seven were for houses for his children and him; the other five were for sale and were worth, according to him, between $185,000 and $227,500.

The subdivision had no substantial environmental obstacles: The soil was good and there were no steep slopes or drainage problems. The developer sought subdivision waivers for sidewalks and to off-center a road in order to save some trees. In addition, the planning board asked him to request a variance on one lot for smaller road frontage, which he did. He used only an attorney and an engineer in the approval process and had no problem getting back his escrow.

It took seven months to get preliminary approval. He estimated that the cost of getting through the planning board process was $67,000. The plans had to be redrawn ten times, even though he believed they were complete. Without those "unnecessary" revisions, he estimates the process would have cost $20,000, so his excess cost was $47,000. He did concede, however, that the subdivision was better drawn as a result of the multiple iterations.

As to regulation after approvals, he had no complaints, noting that building inspectors all have their pet peeves. "When you build in a town, you need to know these, and meet them," he said. Mendham has a very tough fire marshal, but he really does follow the rules. He isn't doing anything wrong, he's just strict."

Developer II

This builder has been in business since 1973. He runs a vertically integrated operation: a realty company to sell his own houses; an excavating business for road and site work on his properties; and an engineering firm and a sewer plant for his projects. He has built several subdivisions in Morris and Union Counties with the help of his wife and several long-term key employees.

The development we spoke to him about was a 492-acre site that had been approved for ninety-eight units, of which eighty-six were to be single-family homes on one-and-one-quarter-acre sites. The other twelve units were to be two sixplexes of affordable condominium housing. The homeowners were to own fifty acres around the site's lake, and 310 acres were to be owned by a private conservation group and open to the public.

The developer said the site was "not virgin land in any sense. It was a Boy Scout center, with numerous buildings and improvements. There were some homeless squatters and abandoned buildings on the site." Indeed, the site had quite a local history. At one time AT&T had intended to build a conference center on it, but the town objected, so a conservation center bought it. That use didn't work out either, so the land was sold to a builder who got preliminary subdivision approval in 1987. Eventually, however, that builder gave a deed-in-lieu to a bank, which in turn sold it to the developer we interviewed.

When that developer bought the property, he had two expectations: that the development would be a godsend to Mendham in meeting its COAH *Mount Laurel* obligations and that he would be building homes within one year. When we interviewed him in April 1996, however, he was just beginning to build—two years later than he had anticipated.

He had faced several problems. First, although he had a valid U.S. Army Corps of Engineers permit, he had to perform a historical and cultural survey of the entire tract because he needed to fill a quarter-acre of wetlands. The New Jersey Department of Environmental Protection mandated the study based on its understanding of its responsibility under its delegated authority to enforce the 1986 Freshwater Wetlands Protection Act. According to DEP, the survey was required because there were eight abandoned buildings on the site. Had he not needed to fill that quarter-acre of wetlands, he simply could have torn them down.

Because of that DEP action, the builder estimated unanticipated carrying costs of between $1 million and $2 million. He attributed that number to taxes—about $300 per day—and to the cost of capital and bank borrowings for holding the land.

Another problem occurred in 1993 when a citizens group attempted to overturn the project's initial approvals. The group maintained that there was ambiguity in changing wetlands and other environmental regulations, particularly related to grandfathering and permit extensions. In response to that citizen concern, the township asked the developer to prepare a new environmental impact statement (EIS), which cost more than $100,000. It was about fourteen inches thick and was, according to the developer, essentially the same as the one-and-a-half-inch-thick one prepared for the original builder.

As part of the process, he also had to pay in excess of $100,000 to the township consultants who were reexamining the project. He calculated that those consultants cost him $600 an hour at planning board meetings.

The builder also had to do a $3,000 study to show that the site had no swamp pink—an endangered plant that grows in a watershed twelve miles away. The builder called that an example of DEP's willingness to believe that conditions are such on a site that some other condition could exist, even if all it has to go on is a remotely credible suggestion. In regard to the swamp pink issue, the planning board member said she would have rather seen the money spent on planting swamp pink in some of the open spaces on the site.

On the whole, this developer's view of regulation in the planning process coincided with that of the planning board member and the board attorney.

NEW JERSEY CASE STUDY

Middletown Township

Middletown Township is a fairly affluent community with a 1995 population of about 65,000. It encompasses 59.4 square miles in Monmouth County. In 1990, the median family income was $60,714. It is mostly built out now, having undergone substantial growth since the 1950s. We interviewed the director of planning, the town engineer, a developer active in the area, and an attorney who works with builders in Middletown.

The Planning Board

The attorney asserted that there is a political dimension to planning board member selection, and that the process is controlled by the Republican party. The town planning director agreed that "it is a very political process." He said, though, that there have been Democrats on the board, and that there is no correlation between land-use decisions and political party affiliation.

On a scale of 1 to 5, where 1 is purely technical and 5 is purely political, the engineer and the planning director both rated the decision-making process as a 2. The lawyer concurred, giving it a 2 or a 3. The developer didn't rate the process at all. He believed decisions are "hard to generalize—they are really made on a case-by-case basis—some decisions are more political than others, some are entirely professional." Several people we interviewed detailed what they considered a politically motivated zoning change. The AT&T facility in Middletown wanted a zoning change to accommodate additional office space and said it would leave the area if it was not forthcoming. It got its change. The developer also noted that decisions are sometimes controlled by board members' personal idiosyncrasies. For example, he said, the chair of the planning board tends to oppose cul-de-sacs because he is an advocate of firefighters.

When asked what impact the public had on planning board decisions, the developer said "a significant voice." He expanded that thought this way: "Large public interest can shape planning board decisions. It may hold a special hearing for the public to voice thoughts."

The planning director believed that mayors should be excluded from planning boards, since planning boards are not supposed to be political bodies, and mayors are directly accountable to the public.

The developer mentioned another political dimension of the planning board. He believed that it was a "negative" for him to use consultants who are municipal engineers in other places. "Petty politics tend to emerge: They are made to jump through more hoops than an unattached professional."

The Application Process

Middletown has an informal review process, but an applicant must request it. The attorney thought it useful to have feedback before any hearing. He said that an informal review is particularly useful for builders/ developers who have a good reason to deviate from the zoning plan or master plan. If there is a rationale behind a proposed change, the planning board will, he believed, generally go along with it. He always suggests to his clients that they go through the informal review. He said, however, that the town engineer doesn't like to do informal reviews before fees are paid because there is no one to bill. Once fees are paid, the engineer is happy to participate in the process.

The developer said that builders are encouraged to coordinate with the planning department up front, prior to going before the planning board, and that he generally discusses projects with the planning department well before starting a formal application process. He is aware of what his firm is entitled to in regard to zoning and the master plan, and he lets it be known that he will sue if denied approvals unjustly. He asserted that with that understanding, he rarely has a problem.

Builders generally bring fully engineered plans to the planning board, even though most of the members cannot read engineering plans, according to the attorney. The town engineer determines whether an application is complete, using an extensive checklist. Then the planning department does another, less complex review.

Both the builder and the lawyer maintained that the approval process is more streamlined in Middletown than in other towns. The lawyer did state that there is often a delay in getting an application on the board's agenda, but that once on, it goes through in a timely manner. Mandated deadlines are usually met, and when extensions are requested, it is generally for good reasons—an unusually complex project, for example. He suggested that the process could be made even better by utilizing a technical review by the professionals and the builder. That way the planning board would have to become involved only when variances are required.

Builders generally receive feedback five or six days before the planning board meeting at which a project will be considered. The builder said that if that notification points out any problems, his firm will pull the project until he can address the issues and resubmit the plan.

Middletown charges application fees for subdivisions. Planning review fees are paid by the municipality, not the developers. Engineering reviews are paid for out of developer-supplied, town-mandated escrow accounts. Professional services fees are also established by ordinance; the attorney said that some builders complain about those fees.

In Middletown, approvals are made contingent on state approvals. The engineer said: "[The town] will give contingent approvals, depending on the specific project. Projects affecting wetlands, or those that might require reconfiguration, are required to provide state clarification."

The planning director estimated that more than 90 percent of applications submitted to the planning board are approved. He believes that is because the professional staff works closely with applicants. The attorney concurs: "They have a great staff."

According to the planning director, Middletown receives very few complaints about the speed of its review process. Indeed, he said that most projects go through the preliminary and final approval processes simultaneously. He also said that sometimes small builders and engineers hold up the process by submitting incomplete packages. He thinks that some outside consultants increase their billings by forcing multiple submissions.

Nevertheless, he says,

> Public input is the biggest factor in slowing down applications. Public protest is often outside the scope of land-use law, but planning board members are political beings and listen to citizen views. Sometimes projects are rejected for political interests, but it does not happen frequently. Multiple hearings may be scheduled for projects with large amounts of public interest.

The planning director indicated that Middletown is somewhat proactive in regard to affordable housing.

> Within Middletown Township they used CDBG [Community Development Block Grant] funds to rehabilitate 200 existing units. They have a scattered-site, single-family housing program that supports nonprofit organizations that do spot-construction and sell affordable units through loans that are repaid after sale. Middletown also has three sites with inclusionary zoning that will generate sixty-seven affordable units. Finally, it is creating 125 units for senior citizens in a mixed-use development that will use LIHTCs [Low-Income Housing Tax Credits].

Middletown employs two licensed planners who help identify appropriate affordable-housing sites. They follow and support planning board philosophy: Better you pick the sites for affordable development than wait for a developer to sue and force you to do it.

Middletown adopted a new master plan in 1993. According to the planning director, its creation engendered a good bit of public interest. Twenty to thirty people came out for the adoption hearing; the planning board listened to all of them. The lawyer supports the plan. "Middletown spent an enormous amount of time on the plan; it's very professional. If you go in with plans consistent with the master plan, you'll get approval a majority of the time. The one time you wouldn't is in the face of stronger citizen opposition."

The planning director noted that New Jersey law requires municipalities to reexamine their master plan every six years. Since there is no requirement for that examination to be public, it is a very superficial process. He also mentioned the 1995 New Jersey law that requires public notice for all zoning changes. However, "The law has a key exception: Notification is not required if a zoning change is attached to an adopted reexamination report. So now anytime a town makes a zoning change, it whips out a reexamination report along with it."

Regulatory Reform

The planning director believed that the New Jersey Freshwater Wetlands Protection Act is too broadly written: Virtually any project can be affected. He noted that even a homeowner looking to build a deck on a house that has a stream nearby will have to go to the state for a wetlands delineation, which can cost as much as the project. Homeowners obviously resent that requirement. The attorney resented the fact that DEP encourages those homeowners to direct their ire at their local communities, even though environmental issues are a matter of state regulation. "It's their law," he said. He believed that the entire regulatory process would be improved if the state delegated some reviews—especially environmental ones—to local planning boards.

The builder made a similar suggestion for regulatory reform. He stated that the sewer approval process should be overseen by a local engineer. "That would speed up the process, and the engineer could be accountable. If something was wrong, he could be fined, or lose his license."

In addition to his idea of delegating environmental decisions, the lawyer had two major suggestions for regulatory reform in New Jersey. First, he would like to see the creation of a land court. "We need to be able to fast-track cases with land use, and we need judges with experience in those cases. That way builders wouldn't be held up for years, sometimes put out of business even if they [should] win their case, just because of the costs of time delay. As the situation stands, you can get a judge who has never heard a land-use case before."

Secondly, he thought it would be a good idea to require a technical review process in communities throughout New Jersey. "It would be useful in all projects to just get everyone together around a table to work issues out rather than just do the process of submitting plans and getting review memos back."

The Developer

We discussed with the developer a specific project he had built: a twenty-seven-lot project that came with preliminary approval. Whatever could go wrong, did.

Using the preliminary approvals of the first owner as a base, the developer obtained approvals for fourteen lots in 1991. In 1992, however, the property was bisected by a new sewer-service-area boundary in a water quality management plan. The problem stemmed from the fact that the original approval had been made before the plan was in effect, but no one had noticed it before.

The developer obtained an application to comply with the water quality management plan and returned it to DEP within a week. However, it took an additional ten months to get approval to move the plat line to conform with property lines—and even that took considerable effort and a significant amount of political clout. The builder doesn't believe that the delay was malicious. There simply weren't enough people approving water quality management plans at the state level.

He did think, however, that timing depends on who you're working with at DEP. "Some personnel will work with you reasonably, some won't even let you call them to check on a project. If the regs give them ninety days, they don't want to hear from you until their time is up."

The Costs

Throughout the delay period, the landowner, not the developer, was covering the carrying costs for the project. Under the terms of the land contract, the developer's firm would take the project to final approval, but the seller would reimburse the firm for costs up to $20,000. The process cost considerably more than that.

The developer had to pay about $40,000 extra for drainage improvements. During the delay period, regulations were changed so that the man-made pond they had intended to use for stormwater was deemed a wetland and thus was unusable. They had to construct a drainage facility that would have been unnecessary had there not been a delay.

Overall, the seven-year-long approval process for the project probably cost about $175,000 extra, according to the developer. During that period, the economy picked up in New Jersey, so he wasn't hurt too much by market changes, but he did incur opportunity costs. For all of 1993, for example, he didn't have a job, because he was waiting to move ahead on the project. He estimated that delays cost him about $100,000 in direct costs and about $300,000 for overhead he had to cover while the project was stalled.

While the approval process was unfolding, the developer had to change the original fourteen-lot plan to a twenty-seven-lot plan in order to protect a historic farm and to maintain open space. The twenty-seven lots originally cost approximately $90,000 each; it cost the developer about $30,000 to improve each lot. The improved land, then, cost about $120,000 per lot, plus debt service. The houses sold for between $280,000 and $525,000 each, with an average price of $308,000. Thus, the project was profitable, but according to the developer, only marginally so.

He thought, though, that the delays cost the land seller significantly. For example, the land had been taxed $325 per year as a farm but came off the farm rolls in April 1993 and was taxed as residential land for fourteen months. That cost the owner $30,000 per year in taxes. The seller also paid the $20,000 for the approval process. That was all in addition to the extra $300,000 the land seller paid due to regulatory factors over and above what they should or could have been.

Nevertheless, the builder emphasized that it is hard to pass on additional costs to buyers: There is only so much that buyers will absorb. "Ultimately," he said, "the market determines the selling price for a house, not the builder."

As far as regulation of the construction process itself, the builder had no complaints. He said, "They've gotten better over the years." The town engineers, unlike those in Princeton Township, don't claim to need seventy-two hours of lead time for inspections. He tries to let them know a week in advance about final inspections, but generally, he feels that as long as he does not habitually ask them to come out without giving them reasonable notice, they are willing to work with him if he needs something done quickly. He noted that his is one of the biggest and oldest building firms in town. "It's important to have a good rapport, and I do."

NEW JERSEY CASE STUDY

Mount Laurel Township

Mount Laurel Township is a community in Burlington County, in the Camden–Gloucester–Burlington labor market area of New Jersey. In the late 1970s, it was a farm community; it is now a mixed-use suburban community with a distinct business elite and high-profile corporate facilities including those of Tyco and Bell Atlantic. In 1994, its estimated population was 34,106; it had nearly doubled since 1980. Growth from 1990 to 1994 was approximately 4 percent annually—a healthy, if not dramatic, population increase. The moderate rate of growth was reflected in residential construction activity as well: 138 single-family building permits were issued in the first six months of 1997. Assuming an average household size of three, that translates into an annualized population growth of 2.4 percent. At buildout the population will be approximately 45,000. The township developed from the west and east toward the middle, progressively using up the most developable land. The land that remains vacant would be relatively costly to develop, largely because of wetlands issues.

The community is not the exclusive, large-lot, bedroom suburb that the landmark litigation bearing its name would suggest: Its median household income in 1990 was $50,843, compared to the state's median of $40,927. Mount Laurel is a middle- to upper-middle-income residential and commercial community whose name has come to be synonymous with fights over fiscal zoning and fair housing.

The courts imposed an "overlay zone" in Mount Laurel as a result of the *Mount Laurel* litigation, allowing, in theory, affordable units to be built at higher densities than market units, ostensibly making such construction more attractive to developers. Nonetheless, the volume of *Mount Laurel* units built or in the pipeline—158 as of 1996—was less than the 300 projected in the plans approved by the New Jersey Council on Affordable Housing.

Mount Laurel and Burlington County have a strong business-services sector. Almost 76 percent of the county workforce is in service occupations. Three of the four largest employers in the township are business-service establishments: Automatic Data Processing, Inc. (550 employees), Telenex Corp. (500 workers), Automotive Rentals, Inc. (450 workers), and Okidata (284 employees).

Mount Laurel has an elected five-member governing body. Both the mayor and the deputy mayor are drawn from that group, which also appoints the nine members of the planning board: the mayor, the manager, a council member, and six at-large individuals. In the mid-1980s, all elected local officials were Democrats; in 1996, all were Republicans.

Insights from Surveys and Interviews

We interviewed the township engineer, its planner, manager, community development director, and a member of the planning board, as well as two developers who have worked in and around the community for several years. We formed the general impression that most of the recent development in Mount Laurel has proceeded with no "unusual" delays or controversy: unusual, that is, within Mount Laurel's historic regulatory context. In general, the process is less dilatory than in bedroom communities near New York. There have been a few contentious projects, with lengthy delays and the threat of legal action, but they seem more the exception than the rule.

All but one of the interviewees indicated that the planning board's reviews of proposed projects were either evenly weighted between technical and political considerations or slightly skewed in the technical direction. One respondent characterized the process as having two vetoes: technical and political. The former occurs when design, environmental, traffic, or related expectations are not being met. The latter occurs when they are substantially met but a citizens group finds fault with a proposal anyway and mobilizes public opposition.

Based on their experiences, the developers differed in their assessment of the planning board. One had difficulty getting approval for a project that contained a mix of units, including some that would help satisfy Mount Laurel's affordable housing needs. He complained that the ninety-day review period specified in New Jersey's Municipal Land Use Law for projects the size of his was systematically circumvented. He claimed that the planning board gave last-minute citizen input undue weight and at the eleventh hour required further explanation or modification. Then, he said, the planning board would "blackmail" him: threaten to deny the plan or to reconsider it beyond the ninety-day period. He also questioned the efficacy of overlay zoning as a means to increase the number of affordable units. He would prefer "zoning by right," so that any proposed affordable housing component proposed would be allowed.

The role of citizen opposition came up in all our interviews. The professionals working for the township conceded that New Jersey municipalities tend to favor the public by not limiting the time citizens are given to comment or requiring them to pay for studies. Yet those professionals also believed that citizen input was a critical check and balance and often caught environmental, design, and traffic problems overlooked by township professionals. Several interviewees suggested planning board members tend to give citizen opposition exaggerated attention for political reasons: to prove they are not "in bed with the developers."

The second developer we interviewed had built more than 6,000 units in the vicinity of Mount Laurel in the past two decades. He complimented the township's professional staff, saying he found "the process of getting through approvals . . . pretty straightforward at the local level." He did point out some bottlenecks the township professionals conceded to. One of those occurred in the 1993–1995 period, when Mount Laurel's building inspection department experienced problems that have since been corrected. Another was the municipal utilities authority, which delayed expanding sewer capacity in the early 1990s, requiring builders to create a diversion line to Mount Holly. Although the sewer capacity was eventually enlarged, one interviewee suggested that the delay was an intentional act to slow down the rate of development. Ninety percent of residential units are on the main sewer system, for which the township imposes a $2,000-per-unit connection fee. The township also operates under a 5-percent-per-year limit on municipal budget increases, and some of our interviewees believed that the cap has affected the township's desirability as a residential location because of its effect on the quality and quantity of public services and infrastructure.

Most interviewees attributed delays in the approval process to the required multidepartmental and multijurisdictional review. First, there is a preliminary approval period, during which a developer gets clearances from various municipal departments. (Such approvals are not always pro forma. One respondent claimed to have had a project delayed for a year by the local fire marshal, who insisted on a second access to the development; the remedy cost $1,000 per lot.) Once those approvals are secured, the planning board will give its approval subject to clearances from relevant county and state review authorities. For example, if the Department of Environmental Protection or the Department of Transportation wants a change in plans, the developer must come before the planning board again. In addition, Mount Laurel requires DEP approvals to be in hand before developments can tap into the sewer system. Plumbing and electrical inspections during the construction process are done by township employees and paid for by the developer.

Everyone we interviewed agreed that the process was inherently time-consuming, even without major citizen opposition or other unusual problems. One thirty-three-unit project that was presented as "typical" took more than four years to progress from the preliminary application to final approval.

Do Developers Make Profits?

We questioned the developers and examined records to determine whether Mount Laurel's relatively lengthy approval period and other imposed costs affected developers' bottom lines. Our general conclusion is that developers in Mount Laurel have made profits, either by passing the costs of regulation backward to landowners or forward to home buyers.

For example, it is common for the developers to use a sixty-day due-diligence period, during which they can tie up possible land purchases while they conduct environmental tests—perhaps to check for heavy metals, as required by DEP. If, during that time, the developers find problems that would cost more to correct than they expected or are willing to spend, they do not buy the land, or they renegotiate the price. (Of course, they do pay the costs of testing.)

In addition, successful developers have learned to play the market, to acquire land at prices that allow profits. During slow periods, larger, better-capitalized developers often buy already improved lots at a discount from developers who cannot afford to hold unsold parcels. Developers in other locations have acquired discounted land from banks and from the REIT (real estate investment trust). As one Mount Laurel developer said: "We have worked in this community for a long time and know the land market." That developer recently purchased land for significantly below the market rate from another developer who needed to sell quickly.

The following example is drawn from a project under construction in 1996. A developer bought land that had already been given preliminary approval for development. He built twenty single-family houses with a mean sales price of $296,117, which included the cost of construction change orders. The developer's mean cost per unit was $247,813: a 16.3 percent gross profit, or a 10.8 percent profit net of prorated sales and advertising costs. The breakdown of costs included $147,613 for construction and change orders, $20,300 for construction overhead, $10,900 for interest, $27,000 per site for half-acre lots, and $42,000 for site improvements.

Those figures provide some insights about the development process in Mount Laurel. The ratio of lot price to sales price in this case is 0.091. The ratio of site improvements to sales price is 0.142. The developer's costs for construction change orders are 70 percent of what he passes on in the final sales price. The developer achieved his goal in this project of keeping hard costs, not including infrastructure, to less than 50 percent of sales price (49.8 percent).

The cost for land in our example is low relative to the market in Mount Laurel as a result of special circumstances. Approved and improved half-acre lots for another project were purchased for approximately $75,000 per parcel. Assuming the same site improvement costs—$42,000 per lot—the price per approved lot without improvements was $33,000. For yet another project in Mount Laurel, the developer paid $33,000 per lot for raw land. The developer in our example confirmed that he does not put much premium on the existence of preliminary approvals; he has confidence in his ability to get those approvals in a timely and straightforward manner in Mount Laurel. That attitude suggests that added costs are shifted forward in the sales price.

That last observation is important for this study. There is not necessarily a high cost from regulatory delays in New Jersey. Local developers with sufficient capitalization take advantage of their intimate knowledge of land markets and local politics to ensure their own profitability. There are costs, however, from other regulatory requirements that get shifted forward to homebuyers in a market where there is excess demand for housing. In the sample project described above, the developer paid $115 per site for environmental testing, $1,000 per site for a recreation fee, a $2,000-per-unit connection fee, and $1,000 per unit for a second access. In order to maintain a minimum net profit margin of around 10 percent, those costs were passed forward to consumers or backward to land sellers.

The developer who provided information about the sample project estimated that, all told, regulation added 30 percent to the final cost of the product. If the 4.0 multiplier is at work, his costs are increased by 7.5 percent. Since his costs for a typical unit were $247,813, his "baseline" costs without regulation would have been $229,227, or almost $20,000 less per unit. That seems consistent with our other evidence. However, as his own example shows, that $20,000 was not shifted ahead to the consumer entirely via the multiplier but did affect the land market.

NORTH CAROLINA CASE STUDIES

With few exceptions, the development process in North Carolina does not require an extended period of review or entail significant delays, especially when contrasted with what is typical in New Jersey. The case study cities were generally consistent in the time they took to process applications and the requirements they imposed. Chapel Hill is a notable exception; it has a New Jersey-like process, which appears to affect the pace and cost of new housing. As a result, Chapel Hill is of particular interest, especially when compared to Cary and Durham, two neighboring communities whose processes are strikingly different. With the exception of Chapel Hill, approvals in North Carolina are usually secured within six months of initial application. Unless rezoning is involved, most subdivision approvals are granted within three months. Impact fees are regularly levied in all three sample cities in the Research Triangle. The single most substantial fee is a $3,000-per-unit school impact fee in Chapel Hill. Public hearings are required for rezoning in all of the cities but, except in Chapel Hill, are not required for subdivision approvals. The subdivision approval process is technical in nature and related only to compliance in all cases but Chapel Hill, where antigrowth sentiments have contributed to a more onerous approval process.

NORTH CAROLINA CASE STUDY

Chapel Hill

Chapel Hill, a town of about 42,000 population in 1995, is one of North Carolina's most affluent communities. In 1990, the median household income was $50,133. Although its economy and culture are driven by the University of North Carolina (UNC) and the UNC hospitals, Chapel Hill is also becoming a bedroom community for Research Triangle Park. The quality of the local public school system is helping to create a demand for housing unmet by local development activity. Indeed, Chapel Hill has the slowest growth of the North Carolina case study cities, with only a 19.4 percent increase from 1980 to 1990.

Chapel Hill's land-use mix is dominated by residential and institutional uses. The town planning department estimates the land uses as follows: 32 percent residential; 23 percent institutional; 16 percent vacant; 12 percent road right-of-way; 10 percent open space; 5 percent office and commercial; and 2 percent agricultural. The predominance of residential and nontaxable institutional uses has strained the town's finances and resulted in a relatively high tax rate: The 1996 tax rate was $.596 per $100, plus an additional $.19 school tax and $.9975 county tax levy. The total assessed value of property in Chapel Hill is $2,186,000,000, or about $49,000 per capita. Local residents and officials are increasingly concerned that Chapel Hill's tax base is too residential.

Chapel Hill has a shortage of land suitable for development. It borders Durham to the east and Carrboro to the west. The topography of the land to the north and south limits growth; expansion would necessitate a substantial investment in water and sewer facilities. Such investment has been ruled out to the north; the town council has established a rural buffer there. Within town limits, much of the land is steep, contains wetlands, or has other constraints. As a result, developers increasingly are turning to environmentally sensitive land for development. Chapel Hill's planning director projects that the town will reach buildout in the year 2020, with a population of 70,000 to 80,000.

Given citizen concern and land scarcity, developers in Chapel Hill are facing an increasingly hostile approval process. The town council has significant oversight in the development process. For example, subdivision proposals for four or more lots require town council approval. In addition, most zoning classifications require a special-use permit for a specific development proposal. According to the town's planning director, the usual time for subdivision approval is eleven to fourteen months if zoning changes are not required. The longest subdivision review process to date took two years.

The approval process includes a mandatory review by the planning board and the transportation board. In addition, some subdivisions are reviewed by the design review board, the parks and recreation board, and/or the greenways review board. Rezoning adds additional time to the process, and as a result, developers in Chapel Hill almost always work within existing zoning. The planning director noted a recent exception in which a subdivision plan required rezoning. The proposal has been under review for more than eighteen months and has not yet received final approval.

One of the most significant barriers to development in Chapel Hill is the town council's limited schedule of public meetings: It holds only nine meetings a year devoted to development. On average, only three development items are placed on the agenda per meeting, and proposals often go before the town council several times to receive final approval, particularly if citizen support is tenuous. According to a local developer, the then current delay for scheduling an item for a first hearing was one year. The approval procedure could be streamlined by granting greater authority for administrative approvals, but the council is not interested in delegating approvals to staff or to the planning board.

Developers noted the burdensome nature of regulations: a steep-slope ordinance; a tree ordinance; resource conservation districts; recreation space requirements, and local water authority guidelines. In addition, there is a $3,000 school impact fee, as well as fees imposed by the local water authority. Developers noted that those regulations add to the cost of development; the costs, however, were all passed on to home buyers. For example, one developer said that when Orange County enacted an additional $1,500 school impact fee for new homes in the Chapel Hill/Carrboro school system, he immediately raised the prices of his houses by $2,000. Developers also said that the value of land in town has declined due to the uncertainty of the approval process. At least one of the developers bases the price paid for land on ordinances affecting the site and will offer a lower price if regulations reduce the potential for development.

According to Chapel Hill's planning director and area developers, much of the delay in the approval process is the result of local opposition.

Consequently, developers make an effort to discuss plans with adjacent landowners both before and during the development process. In fact, one developer said that the first step she takes in the development process is contacting neighbors of a proposed development.

The town's many regulatory requirements notwithstanding, all of the developers we interviewed contended that time is the greatest cost of development in Chapel Hill. The slow process makes it difficult to estimate the demand for housing and adds to the risk of a project. That added risk drives up the cost of capital for local projects.

Developer I

This developer targets the high-end housing market but is involved only in development activities; she does not build homes. All her lots are sold to builders of custom houses. In the past five years, she had developed about 200 lots and is currently developing another thirty-six in a small subdivision. She chooses to work in Chapel Hill because she is successful there. She understands the process and has little competition from developers frightened by the restrictive development process.

She discussed with us the recent approval process for a 400-acre parcel she had purchased for $1.8 million—about $4,500 an acre—from a seller who went bankrupt after the town downzoned the land to one unit per five acres. Due to steep slopes, streams, and the need to establish a significant buffer to the adjacent UNC Botanical Gardens, the parcel has a very limited number of buildable sites. She intended to develop ten one-acre lots on the site and price them from $100,000 to $150,000.

Developer II

In the early 1990s, Chapel Hill passed a small-area plan for its southern section. The plan, covering 2,800 acres, recommended concentrating development around a "town center." The developer to whom we spoke worked for a limited partnership that was established specifically to build clustered development on a 312-acre site in that area. In 1992, the partnership paid approximately $11,000 per acre for that site. Lot sizes range from one-tenth of an acre to one-half of an acre, with the most common being one-sixth of an acre. The developers planned to build apartments, condominiums, and office and commercial space. In addition, 112 acres would remain undeveloped as a resource conservation district. Houses would be priced in the low $200,000 range, town houses at up to $150,000, and condominiums at slightly more than $100,000. According to the developer, most of the lot cost was tied to infrastructure.

Initial plans for the development were submitted in December 1992 and approved in July 1993, with final approvals granted in November of that year. That approval phase covered the first 200 homes and an adjacent commercial site. The approval of a second phase took longer: initial submission in February 1995; approval in May 1996.

The developer faced a few significant obstacles. First, local regulations created some technical compliance problems related to maximum densities. Second, the original plan for stormwater management was not feasible, and the developer had to modify it. Finally, Chapel Hill commissioned a study—at the request of a citizens group—to determine if the development would meet the goals of the small-area plan.

In the process of obtaining approvals, the partnership donated a parcel of land on the site to the local school system for an elementary school. In addition, it agreed to construct a greenway to connect the development to the university. The development is subject to the $3,000 school impact fee. The local water authority charges a $3,000-per-unit tap fee in addition to the hard costs of water and sewer lines. Finally, performance bonds are required to ensure that infrastructure will be completed.

The developer contended that delays in the approval process lowered the return on this Chapel Hill development relative to others in neighboring jurisdictions. It is difficult to predict the final return on the project, but the developer conceded that experience with the development process in Chapel Hill would allow for more success in later ventures.

Developer III

This development company focuses its efforts in Durham and Chapel Hill. In the mid-1990s, it shifted from the entry-level market to the move-up market and was developing a subdivision that had been plagued with difficulties—primarily due to citizen opposition. In total, the approval process took about three years. After the land was partially cleared for infrastructure, a citizen reported to the planning board that the site was once a slave burial ground. The developer had to hire an archaeologist to investigate the claim, which turned out to be false. In addition, the town denied the developer's request to connect the sales-center driveway to the road next to the site. The developer deemed that denial "harassment."

Nonetheless, he was selling lots and building houses. Lots cost about $36,000, with home prices advertised to start in the $170,000 range. The developer conceded that there would be few in that range; most would be priced higher. He went on to state that the houses he was building in Chapel

Hill would cost $35,000 to $40,000 more than the same houses in neighboring Durham. In his words, "You can put up a pup tent in Chapel Hill and sell it for $100,000." He contended that most of the cost difference was due to a diminished supply of new homes in Chapel Hill resulting from the difficult approval process.

Key Issues

Key issues raised during our discussions included the need for Chapel Hill to streamline its approval process, the increasing citizen opposition to new growth, and problems with the local tax base. Chapel Hill's approval process discourages developers from working within the town's planning jurisdiction. The result is a reduced availability of new homes and, consequently, average prices higher than in neighboring jurisdictions. Specific problems include a town council schedule that limits the total number of development items that may be heard in any given year. Then, too, town council members are easily persuaded by citizen opposition. Some officials and citizens are also concerned that opposition to development and the resultant low ratio of commercial to residential development have reduced the tax base and increased the tax burden on local residents.

Conclusion

Chapel Hill is a classic example of a town that is using "planning" as a justification for limiting growth. Delays and difficulties in obtaining approvals have discouraged many developers from entering the market, despite a high demand for new housing. Homes that are constructed within the town limits often yield a higher price than equivalent developments in neighboring jurisdictions.

All three of the local developers we interviewed contended that the development process in Chapel Hill is cumbersome. However, two of them have determined that the process actually benefits some developers. Given the high demand for housing in Chapel Hill and the protracted approval process that limits housing opportunities, the supply of housing in the market does not meet demand. The difficult review process also reduces demand for available land due to the limited number of developers willing to work within Chapel Hill's planning jurisdiction. Consequently, land prices are relatively low, and few competitors exist in the market. The result is a higher rate of return for developers successful in the process and higher home prices for buyers seeking access.

NORTH CAROLINA CASE STUDY

Cary

The "boom town" of Cary, located near Research Triangle Park, is rapidly becoming one of the largest cities in the Raleigh/Durham metropolitan region; its population nearly doubled between 1980 and 1990. The 1994 population was estimated to be 61,439.

Cary has a relatively healthy mix of residential and nonresidential uses, with the current split estimated at roughly 60 percent residential and 40 percent nonresidential. In 1995, Cary's total valuation was estimated at $3,590,000,000, or about $58,000 per person. Its tax rate as of 1996 was $.54 per $100 assessment, with an additional $.76 levied by the county.

In November 1999, Cary's voters elected a slower-growth majority to city council for the first time in town history. Until then, the town was unabashedly development-friendly, with the council and planning department working closely with developers. (One developer stated that council members have actually apologized when the approval process has resulted in delays of just thirty days.) At the time we conducted the case study, Cary was reorganizing its planning, engineering, and construction management departments into a single "development services" division. According to the town's planning director, that and other reforms are intended "to better serve the development community." In fact, the town is holding focus groups with developers to determine the best methods of reform.

Cary has two distinct processes for rezoning and subdivision approval. Proposals that require a rezoning must go through a rezoning procedure before the subdivision review process begins. Currently, that process requires a technical review by town departments. Next, a combined public hearing is held for both the council and the planning and zoning board. The proposal is reviewed again by staff before the board votes. Only then does the city council vote on the proposal. The subdivision review procedure follows a similar process, with the addition of a review by the appearance commission. No public hearings are required.

Cary has established a timetable for rezoning and subdivision approvals: just over four months. The typical zoning approval process takes sixty days, and the subdivision review process takes about seventy-five days. According to local developers, it takes about six months from the date of land purchase to a project's start and another six to eight months for infrastructure development. Within a year, builders are able to begin the construction of new homes. Cary has also published a schedule with specific timetables for submission, review, public hearings, and council votes. That schedule allows developers to know exactly how long the entire approval process will take.

Developers in Cary indicated that the town clearly defines requirements and that the process is certain. Consequently, they are able to predict costs; their only uncertainty rests with the economy. However, the quick approval process allows developers to respond rapidly to market conditions.

Cary does add some development costs, although most have been included in impact fees: a transportation fee; an acreage fee to support water and sewer services; connection fees; and recreation fees. One developer provided an example of a unit where fees were $4,600 for development and another $1,947 for construction. That figure included all permits, water and sewer fees, inspection fees, and road improvements. Cary also requires more landscaping than other jurisdictions in the area but does not require open space set-asides or sidewalks. The town follows state guidelines for most environmental regulations.

Developer I

The first developer to whom we spoke had been in business in Cary for nearly eighteen years and had developed approximately 6,000 lots in that time. He targets the move-up market, sells lots to builders, and allows only one real estate company to market homes built in his developments.

In his most recent development, homes sold from the mid-$200,000s to the mid-$300,000s. He could not provide specific cost-per-unit estimates of regulatory requirements. He did, however, believe that meeting local regulations costs between $2,800 and $4,200 per unit, or about 1 to 2 percent of the final sales price. That figure does not include additional costs imposed during the construction phase. He is concerned that increasing opposition to growth, fueled by school overcrowding, may slow the approval process in Cary. He said he is willing to support a school impact fee of as much as $4,000 to $5,000 to quell this opposition.

Developer II

This developer operates primarily in the Raleigh/Durham metropolitan area and recently developed a subdivision of 142 homes in Cary. Prices ranged from $205,000 to $210,000 for 2,000- to 3,000-square-foot houses.

The developer bought the subdivision plan with preliminary approvals in place, so he did not carry out the entire approval process. He was able, however, to estimate the costs of regulations and fees at $4,599 per lot for development and $1,947 per lot for construction: $6,546, or about 3 percent of the cost of each house. More than half of the development costs were related to transportation improvements required on roadways adjacent to the property. Water and sewer inspection fees and assessments represented about 13 percent of the development costs and more than half of the construction phase costs.

Key Issues

At least one major developer working in Cary is concerned that citizen opposition to development may jeopardize the current approval process. Developers also expressed frustration with the contradictory recommendations they receive from agencies in Cary. The town is addressing that concern by consolidating several related departments into a single organization that will control the approval process.

Conclusion

Cary has been one of the most rapidly growing cities in North Carolina. Until recently, it opened its doors wide to new development and made every effort to help developers walk through. Although it has a relatively low property tax rate and a healthy tax base, its future is not clear. Rapid growth has placed some strain on the local school system, leading to increased opposition to new growth. Overall, however, the two developers interviewed in Cary were happy with the approval process. It allows them to respond quickly to market conditions.

NORTH CAROLINA CASE STUDY

Durham

Durham is located in the center of the Raleigh/Durham metropolitan area in Durham County. It is immediately adjacent to Research Triangle Park, and its major employment centers include its downtown and Duke University. Durham consolidated predominantly white (suburban) and black (inner-city) school districts in 1992. The uncertainty surrounding that process, and a relatively high crime rate in the city, made Durham less attractive as a residential location in the early to mid-1990s than adjacent municipalities. The situation has improved recently, however, as the town has grown to 136,611 residents with a median household income of $21,547, the seventh highest in North Carolina. The city has a high tax rate relative to other counties in the state: $.68 per $100 assessed value.

At the county level, Durham still has significant agricultural use and open space. The planning department's most recent estimate of land use says the mix is 40 percent agricultural, 28 percent open space, 18 percent residential, 4 percent commercial, 4 percent institutional, 4 percent other, and 2 percent unclassified.

The planning departments in Durham City and Durham County recently merged into a single organization with jurisdiction over the entire county. The board attempts to streamline the development process by running rezoning and subdivision approval processes concurrently and by setting timetables for the approval process. The result is a process that allows for full approvals in four to five months, even when rezoning is required. According to the planning director, about 50 percent of rezoning petitions are approved. Denials most commonly result from organized citizen opposition.

If they involve fewer than fifty units, subdivision applications may be approved by the staff and the development review board. Otherwise, the city council or the county commissioners vote on proposals after staff have made recommendations. Approval is determined in large part by the results of technical reviews conducted by the city's departments.

Some regulations in Durham are more restrictive than those in other case study cities. For example, Durham regulates development within watersheds at a level beyond the state minimums. Durham also assesses some impact fees, including a recreation fee, a transportation fee, and water and sewer fees. In total, those fees average between $1,300 and $2,000 per unit.

One developer provided us with details about a particular development where total fees reached about $2,765 per constructed unit: $1,300 per lot for development and $1,465 at the building stage. The total included all water and sewer, transportation, recreation, open space, water meter, and building permit fees. Of that total, more than 60 percent of costs were related to water and sewer connections and fees.

Durham developers contend that regulations and the approval process do not significantly affect the target market or prices.

Developer I

We interviewed the development manager of a firm that recently switched from the entry-level to the move-up market in both Durham and Chapel Hill. Most recently, the firm developed a 37.4-acre, sixty-eight–unit subdivision in Durham priced in the low $200,000s for 2,000- to 3,000-square-foot homes. The land was purchased for a little more than $20,000 per acre under an agreement that required approval of all permits for development before the transaction occurred.

Total impact fees in this subdivision were about $758 per unit. The construction phase added another $1,273 per home, all related to water and sewer fees. The total costs were $2,031, or about 1 percent of the final home price. That total does not include additional costs imposed by the required installation of sidewalks, curbs, and gutters, but the developer did not provide us with a specific per-unit cost for those requirements.

Developer II

This developer, who builds about 100 houses each year, traditionally targeted the entry-level buyer with some of the lowest-priced homes in Durham. His firm recently shifted its focus to the move-up market, with homes priced at about $150,000. He contended that the Durham planning process does not significantly affect the final cost of homes. He stated that the total approval process typically takes less than six months, which allows him to react quickly to changing markets and reduces his risks in undertaking a new development project.

Key Issues

The housing market in Durham is softer than in some neighboring jurisdictions, owing in part to perceived instability in the county's school system and higher-than-average crime rates relative to the region. Nonetheless, new home prices in Durham have been rising, more as a consequence of demand than as a result of delay-induced carrying costs.

Conclusion

Durham offers a clear and predictable approval process that drew few criticisms from the developers with whom we spoke. They are pleased with the speed with which it operates and with their interactions with the town's professional planning staff.

 **NORTH CAROLINA CASE STUDY**

Jacksonville

Jacksonville is located in southeastern North Carolina in Onslow County. Its economy is driven by Camp Lejeune, a military base located entirely within its corporate limits. There are few other major employers in the county; most nonmilitary employment is in the service sector. In fact, Onslow County has the ninety-second lowest median household income in North Carolina: $13,168 in 1993. Between 1980 and 1990, Jacksonville's population grew by 327.0 percent, from 18,259 to 78,092; nearly all that increase was due to the annexation of Camp Lejeune.

Jacksonville's housing market is unique to the case study cities in North Carolina in that it is clearly defined by the income level of local military employees. In fact, one local developer interviewed discussed the target market in terms of military rank. Home prices are low: 800-square-foot duplexes sell for $49,500, and single-family houses sell for less than $90,000. Very few homes sell for more than $150,000; those that do are custom built. Many of the county's home buyers finance through Veterans Administration loans.

The development process in Jacksonville is relatively simple. Most developers are required only to receive a subdivision approval, which is reviewed for technical compliance. Zoning districts in Jacksonville allow for a higher density than currently demanded in the residential market, so rezoning is seldom required.

The subdivision review process begins with the submission of a concept plan that is reviewed by the planning department to identify potential problems. Then the applicant submits a detailed plan. Jacksonville's technical advisory committee, made up of representatives from various town departments, evaluates the plan for technical compliance. If the plan meets all local requirements, it goes before the planning board for approval. Finally, the town council votes on the proposal.

The approval process is predictable and nonpolitical. In total, it takes as little as four weeks, but more typically sixty to ninety days. The only impact fees are water and sewer tap fees, as well as a park fee. Sidewalks, curbs, and gutters are also required within Jacksonville's planning jurisdiction.

The Developer

We spoke with the local manager of a family-owned development business that has developed projects in Jacksonville for about thirty years. On average, the company constructs approximately eighty homes per year in Jacksonville and another eighty to 100 in Myrtle Beach, South Carolina. Seventy percent of its homes are single-family; 30 percent are multifamily. It targets moderate-income buyers.

The company was developing a seventy-five–acre tract of land close to Camp Lejeune. The tract served as the company's primary development site for many years and was projected to meet the company's needs for the next twenty. Within that tract, the company was building small duplex houses as well as single-family dwellings on large waterfront lots.

The city of Jacksonville had recently absorbed the company's tract into its planning jurisdiction. The developer concluded that the only difference that has made is that he now must meet additional requirements for sidewalks, curbs, and gutters, as well as heightened paving standards. Sidewalks add approximately $200 to $300 per unit; the other requirements add about $2,000 to $3,000 per unit. In addition, the county charges $400 per unit to tap into the water system. The company has established its own wastewater treatment facility and estimates the per-unit cost of this facility to be $4,000 to $5,000, including all line costs.

The developer hires a local engineering firm to obtain all necessary approvals and estimates that the approval process costs about $400 per unit. That figure includes some design work the engineering firm conducts during the approval process and may therefore overestimate the final cost of obtaining approvals. Environmental regulations, particularly those related to wetlands, have limited the amount of land suitable for development. However, the builder contended that those restrictions would not affect the price of homes. He simply planned to build out his available land at a quicker pace.

Key Issues

Development regulations and fees are not significantly affecting the cost of housing development in Jacksonville. Citizens are not involved in the planning process, and requirements are relatively simple. Developers are most concerned about the long-term health of the area economy. Local commerce leaders are attempting to broaden the economic base to provide additional support. Unless and until the base changes, developers will continue to face a clearly defined market where salaries of military employees determine the final price of their homes.

Conclusion

Overall, the development process in Jacksonville is well defined and one of the quickest of the case study cities. The relative certainty of the approval process allows local developers to hire others to obtain all approvals and keeps the cost of approvals relatively low. That certainty, in addition to the limited cost, allows developers to construct homes at a price that provides even the lowest-paid military employees access to the market.

NORTH CAROLINA CASE STUDY

Concord

Concord, in Cabarrus County, is a rapidly growing city within the Charlotte commuting shed. Population increased from 16,900 in 1980 to 39,200 in 1996, with considerable additional growth projected. Most new construction serves people who commute to Charlotte, but Concord has several large employment centers within its corporate limits: a Philip Morris manufacturing plant; a Fieldcrest-Cannon plant; and Perdue Farms, each of which employs more than 800 people. Concord is also home to the Charlotte Motor Speedway and its associated development. The mix of residential and non-residential use is healthy by conventional planning standards: 57 percent of lands are in residential use, 25 percent in commercial and industrial use, and 18 percent in public use.

The land-use mix is important because of its consequences for public finance. In 1980, for example, the total property tax valuation of the city was approximately $250 million, or $14,800 per capita. Due to growth, annexation, revaluation, and the success of the aforementioned properties, the total in 1996 was close to $3 billion, or approximately $70,000 per capita. Even adjusted for inflation, growth is impressive: from approximately $18,000 to more than $45,000 per capita. Added to that is the fact that Concord is an "electri-city" (i.e., it buys bulk power from Duke Power and sells it at retail prices, which results in a sizable annual benefit). Concord also enjoys considerable revenue from taxes on ticket sales at the Speedway. Finally, Concord is home to a general aviation airport (with a property tax valuation of $12.7 million) at which ninety-nine aircraft are based.

Thus, Concord's growth has not created too much financial pressure to date. Indeed, the city's 1996 tax rate was below what it was in every year before 1990—and at $0.44 per $100 valuation, the rate is among the lowest in the state for urban locales. Even so, there is growing momentum to charge developers more to cover the costs of development approvals.

Quality and Price of Land

While there are relatively few wetland areas in Cabarrus County, there are several streams and ponds that require Department of Environment and Natural Resources (DENR) or Federal Emergency Management Agency (FEMA) approval to cross, as well as erosion and sedimentation control plan approval. The county also has a plethora of bull tallow (yellow clay) soil, which makes a very poor building surface and must be removed and filled. Thus, developers tend to buy the best land first. One of the developers indicated that the land least costly to develop is nearly gone. He recently paid $16,000 per acre for good, buildable land and $7,500 per acre for somewhat improved land that lacks water and sewer infrastructure. The other developer to whom we spoke had recently paid approximately $9,300 per acre for unimproved land that was zoned for intensive use and included allowances for multifamily and commercial development.

Regulatory Costs

There are no growth controls or impact fees in Concord. Developers must pay application fees, but they are negligible. They must also pay a $500-per-unit fee to tap in to sewer mains, but there is no frontage or individual hookup fee. One developer estimated that the total cost of regulatory fees, approvals, and required planning and engineering drawings is less than $500 per unit. He considers that amount such a small fraction of his costs that he does not even track it.

Bonding and Warranties

Bonding requirements are minimal. When a developer records the plat for each phase of a subdivision, he or she is required to post 125 percent of the remaining development costs. That amounts to nothing if the subdivision is fully improved when it is recorded. The builder/contractor is bonded and warranties the installation and operation of infrastructure for one year.

Infrastructure Costs

Both developers stated that their target infrastructure cost per lot was $6,000 to $7,000, including soft costs, permits, and fees. The soft costs are clearly higher in New Jersey, but so are the hard costs—in part, for technical reasons. For example, because the frost line is shallower in North Carolina, it is less costly to excavate for pipes. Also, construction labor is less expensive in North Carolina.

Both men develop only property with water and sewer lines. That requires more expenditure up front and means that some subdivisions must be annexed to the city as part of the development deal.

One of the developers has put in his own package plants and pumping stations in some large projects. His reasoning is that unimproved land not accessible to city water and/or sewage facilities can be bought at substantial discounts ($4,000 to $5,000 per acre), while the facility costs amount to about $1,000 per acre. The total investment, then, is still less than the $10,000 per acre charged for land accessible to water and sewer. Once built, the plants are turned over to homeowner associations to operate. On the downside, DENR must approve package systems, which is burdensome.

The Development Environment

A healthy fiscal situation, much available land, and large, protected tracts have combined to create a supportive development environment in Concord. In addition, both developers considered the Concord planning staff to be highly professional and competent, with an ability to make requirements clear.

The residents of Cabarrus County generally support growth. They have appeared at public hearings, however, to oppose rezonings that would have allowed a truck stop adjacent to a residential neighborhood, and they have expressed concern about the city's ability to provide services in newly annexed areas. A growing number of residents are urging the adoption of impact fees and dedications. According to the town engineer, these people generally have moved to Concord from areas that use such mechanisms.

Approval times are relatively short, in keeping with the supportive development environment. One developer said that approval takes about five to six months from the drawing board to the final approval, which is about as fast as he can go. He does not incur carrying costs during that time, because he purchases options to buy land with expiration dates that would free him if approvals were delayed. Certainly, there is a small markup for options, and if they need to be renewed, there would be associated costs. But that has not happened to him in Concord.

Developers work with the planning department and submit a preliminary subdivision plan for town council approval. After that concept plan is approved, a developer works with the professional planning staff on the details. Only "significant" changes require another hearing, and Concord has a fluid definition of "significant." One developer called that approach "design as you go," noting that as long as proposed changes are "reasonable," they will be approved by the planners.

Both developers agreed that state and federal permits take more time than local approvals. One had to wait nearly nine months for a stream-crossing approval from FEMA. When a developer's plan affects flow in a stream channel, the Corps of Engineers gets involved as well. And DENR weighs in on dam safety when dams—especially those classified as "high hazard"—are constructed. The developer had to wait more than a year to resolve dam projects. He continued to work in the meantime, but those delays might have caused him to miss the market.

Developer I

This man is the managing partner in a three-person firm. He takes 10 percent of the hard costs as his management fee, and all three partners split profits according to their ownership shares. He always controls more than 50 percent of the profits. The group buys and develops land. It confines its activities to Cabarrus County because it knows the rules and the players so well and has been very successful. In 1995 the group brought 250 units to market, and in 1996, it expected to complete 325 units. All the units are single-family and are stick-built, ranging in price from less than $100,000 to more than $250,000. The group has built in small and large subdivisions, as well as in planned-unit developments (PUDs).

The group actively scouts for land, identifying farmers and rural property holders and waiting for them to decide to sell. It always buys land outright from owners, using purchase options to cover the approval period. In large land deals, the group takes land down in pieces over three years, using revenues that flow in from early sales.

The partner spoke to us about a specific ninety-acre tract. The land was purchased in 1988 for $7,500 per acre, using an 8 percent loan. Initially he planned to take the land down over a seven- to eight-year period, but that was accelerated. Eighty of the ninety acres were improved for development and subdivided into 225 lots. The design called for three equal-sized villages, each with homes ranging from $130,000 to $250,000.

The developer sought a rezoning to PUD, motivated by the great flexibility that zoning allows. (Unlike Cary, Concord does not use "conditional zoning" for other than PUD zones.) The rezoning process took four months, which was as fast as he could expect given public notification ordinances.

The economics of the project worked out nicely for the developer. Land costs were $675,000 ($7,500 x 90). Factoring in infrastructure development costs, soft costs associated with approvals, and interest (or opportunity) costs over the length of the time the land was held (at 8 percent), the developed price per lot was approximately $11,000 to $13,000. Assuming he was able to sell each lot for $20,000 to builders, he was netting between 30 and 60 percent return per year—depending on how quickly he closed out the project. That is consistent with his statement that his partnership averages a 50 percent rate of return on its investments.

Developer II

This developer has a background in architecture and design. Our discussion with him reflected a design orientation to development, not merely an interest in the bottom line. He and his partner were in the midst of developing a project with a "neotraditional" design when we interviewed him.

The 123-acre site was not without its problems. The original owner had subdivided a fourteen-acre parcel for a church. The parcel was under a small-area plan that required that it provide employment, not merely residences. Thirty acres were in an unbuildable floodplain. Further, while a highway interchange was planned for a corner of the site, if it were delayed, demand for the commercial space would be affected. Finally, the site was expensive: $9,349 an acre. Despite the drawbacks, the developer bought it. He would make the unbuildable areas open space and hope for timely completion of the interchange. He justified the high cost by considering the high densities at which he could build and the mixed uses he could provide.

The developer sought rezoning to PUD classification and annexation to the city. According to him, that flexibility was the only way to make the development consistent with the small-area plan. The site was divided into pieces: seventy single-family units on sixteen acres; 127 single-family units on thirty-four acres; twenty duplex units on three acres; approximately 300 apartments in a multifamily structure on thirteen acres; and 160,000 square feet of commercial space. Most of the single-family homes would sell for $120,000 to $150,000; those adjacent to the open space would sell for $200,000. The developer expected those homes to be bought by second- and third-time home buyers. The duplex units, 1,300 to 1,400 square feet in size, would be priced at $90,000 to $100,000.

The developer planned to sell the improved residential lots to builders, with covenants to ensure consistency with design standards. He intended to maintain ownership and management control of the multifamily and retail space.

Given the multiple uses planned for the project, it is difficult for us to do a back-of-the envelope calculation of profitability. There are some indicators, however. The project was financed by a bank, which required the loan to be repaid by 75 percent of sellout; that implies a 25 percent total return.

The developer stated that the ratio of sales price to lot price should be in the 16 to 18 percent range. If a house sold for $135,000, the improved lot would have a value of approximately $23,000. If the prorated price of the raw lot was $2,525 (0.27 acres per lot; each acre at $9,349) and the cost per lot of improvements and approvals was $7,000, the lot's price without figuring carrying costs would be just under $10,000. The developer also noted that approvals and associated soft costs are negligible. Assuming construction and land financing at 10 percent over three years, the developer's basis in the improved lot would be close to $15,000. Using those numbers, the annualized rate of return would be approximately 18 percent.

Key Issues

Two issues came up repeatedly in the course of this case study: the need to change the way development is financed and the consequences of growth on the quality of life in Concord.

In March 1996, Concord commissioned "Capital Costs Due to Growth," a study by Tischler and Associates. The authors estimated that a new single-family unit in transitional areas in and around Concord (i.e., not rural, not urban core), generated $18,522 in infrastructure costs, broken down as follows: $8,067 for schools; $6,019 for water and wastewater; $4,033 for state roads; and $403 for recreation and EMS vehicles. Costs generated by single-family units in rural areas and by multifamily units in the urban core were lower ($7,163 and $3,332, respectively).

Of those costs, education is the most controversial, because it, along with recreation, does not have a dedicated revenue stream to pay off revenue bonds. Traditionally, the local cost of education is paid from general revenues, mostly from property taxes.

A residential unit with a tax value of $125,000 would pay $550 per year in property taxes. The report estimates that elementary school operating costs per year, per household, are $58.45. Capital costs are estimated to total approximately $3,200 per household. Assuming a life of 30 years and an 8 percent mortgage rate, that translates into $284 per year per household. Thus, the annual costs per household are in the $342 range. Of course, that new housing unit also has to pay for police and fire protection, libraries, recreation, and other facilities and services that may not have user fees.

New construction does not seem to add an enormous burden, at least not in Cabarrus County. Nonetheless, there is the perception that it does, and support is building for an impact fee, a realty transfer fee, a supplemental property tax for schools, a dedication of part of the local-option sales tax for schools, or growth controls, including downzoning, open space dedications, an adequate public facilities ordinance, or development exactions.

Not surprisingly, the developers we interviewed opposed all these options, especially an impact fee, on equity grounds. One of them asserted that only newcomers to the area would be likely to support these ideas.

There was remarkably little concern about the congestion and environmental problems that inevitably accompany rapid growth. Currently, there is no interest in developing commuter bus service to Charlotte, although it could ease congestion and pollution. In fact, several new road projects are either under way or in the planning stage.

7

Implications for Policy

We began this study by admitting our predilection that regulation is costly. Common logic suggests that someone pays for the time and effort necessary to follow specified procedures and to install particular improvements deemed essential for health, safety, and environmental quality. The literature confirms that regulations have a cost but tends to be anecdotal and case-specific. Moreover, methodological problems have compromised the precision of previous estimates of the cost of regulation.

We have advanced the literature both conceptually and methodologically. Conceptually, we have clarified the types of costs that regulation creates, distinguished "normal" from "excessive" regulatory costs, and elaborated a decision model to help us understand the incidence of the regulatory costs in both the short and long runs.

The very nature of the residential development sector makes data collection difficult. Despite our best efforts, we ran into many of the same methodological problems as did others. However, by triangulating the problem, processing the survey data we were able to collect, conducting case studies, and performing statistical analysis, we believe we have shed more light on the topic than any of our predecessors.

Three key questions motivated this project:

1. *How much do different kinds of regulation contribute to the cost of new residential development?*

2. *How are the costs of regulation distributed among buyers, developers, and landowners in the short and long runs?*

3. *What are the consequences of those costs for residential construction?*

Answers to these questions are contained in the review of the literature (chapter 2) and in subsequent chapters. In this chapter, we pull the evidence together and ask what it means for policy.

THE COST OF REGULATION

In chapter 1 we distinguished normal from excessive regulatory costs. The former were defined as outlays on regulations that might be considered "reasonable" or "necessary" in order to achieve commonly agreed upon goals—such as the preservation of health, safety, and environmental quality—and costs incurred to comply with regulations in a "reasonable" period of time. The latter were stipulated to be outlays on regulations deemed to be "excessive" substantively: those that require developers to incur more hard costs than they would in some baseline case, as well as costs incurred due to unnecessary delays.

We decided to stress excessive costs for two reasons. First, we believed that those costs were the most appropriate targets for policy. Stakeholders will argue whether some of what we define as "normal" regulation is necessary, but we wanted to eliminate any discussion of common zoning and subdivision practices, or of regulations that protect environmental quality. On the other hand, few would disagree that "excessive" regulation should be curtailed.[29] Our approach allows us to avoid what the literature refers to as "amenity" consequences of regulation: an increase in land values due to regulations that make a specific location more attractive by reducing residential densities, for example, or by requiring large buffers. Developers are willing to pay more for land in those cases, knowing that they can pass costs on to buyers. In our approach, regulation has only a negative effect on land values, as one possible response by developers to the burden they face. Any observed increases in final home sales prices, then, are due to the regulatory costs only.

We broke down excessive regulatory costs into five types:

1. *Opportunity costs of restricted land use*

2. *Hard costs* associated with the bricks and mortar necessary to meet requirements

3. *Soft costs*, including outlays for legal, planning, architecture, engineering, and environmental consulting, title searches, and surveying—all required to develop an application

4. Related *out-of-pocket fees* that must accompany applications

5. *Opportunity costs from delays* that a regulatory approval process creates

Opportunity and hard costs result from subdivision, zoning, and environmental regulations. In tables 11–13 (see chapter 5), we list the major requirements of those ordinances, which can add a total of approximately $38,375 to the cost of a home in New Jersey (adding up median responses).

Based on interviews with developers, local engineers, and planners, we can judge a subset of those requirements to be "discretionary," if not nonessential. Therefore, by our definition, they constitute excessive costs. For example, tree ordinances are reported to add $500 per unit to developers' costs; negotiated open space set-asides add another $3,500 per unit; restrictions on clustering have a median cost of $2,000 per unit; bond-release difficulties cost $500 per unit; and discretionary planning board decisions have a median price of $1,000 per unit. Those discretionary or nonessential elements may not all be present in a single municipality, and the cost they add in different municipalities undoubtedly varies around the median. Indeed, as table 20 shows, there are systematic differences in the regulatory environment in New Jersey. Nonetheless, we can use those figures to provide an order of magnitude for *the per-unit cost of substantive regulatory requirements that are not necessarily needed for health, safety, and environmental protection: approximately $7,500 per unit.*

In addition, there are out-of-pocket costs of regulation in the form of application fees. The mean costs of those for subdivision, rezoning, environmental, and fair-share housing plan review sum to almost $3,000 per unit in New Jersey, according to survey respondents. One can debate whether those fees are necessary. Municipalities claim that they are levied mostly to offset processing costs. However, many municipalities that charge application fees also charge an applicant for the time staff or outside consultants spend reviewing plans. The sum of those mean costs was almost

$7,000 per unit in New Jersey. Out-of-pocket application and review costs, therefore, total $10,000.

The application and review costs assessed builders and developers in New Jersey are far higher than in North Carolina, where there are modest application fees and no tradition of municipalities charging applicants for review time. Those costs are paid out of general revenues.

We conclude, therefore, that a portion of the approximately $10,000 per-unit application and review costs paid by New Jersey developers is excessive. The costs borne by builders/developers for plans and specifications (approximately $9,000 per unit) also seem inflated in New Jersey compared to North Carolina, since municipalities in New Jersey tend to require more detailed information as a condition for approval, and multiple reviews require several iterations of those formal plans and specifications.

To judge whether $19,000 in plan preparation, review, and application costs and fees is "excessive" requires the application of some norm. In North Carolina, the comparable costs and fees are $9,500 per unit, suggesting that *New Jersey's per-unit costs and fees are too high by $9,500.*

Next, we can discuss the costs that arise as a consequence of excessive time delays. We reported in chapter 3 that subdivision waivers and variances took twelve months and zoning-change applications took fourteen months for the median respondent in New Jersey, and that the average median time for environmental reviews was approximately 8.4 months (taking the mean of medians for six types of review).

Builders/developers claim that those review periods are excessive: some 7.5 months for subdivision waivers and variances; 9.5 months for rezonings; and 1.2 months for environmental reviews. Regulators generally believe that review times are reasonable, given the pressures that exist. The difference between builders'/developers' and regulators' responses reflects different perspectives, as well as the fact that the two groups seem to count elapsed time differently.

The overview of procedural requirements in New Jersey contained in chapter 3 suggests that reviews could be done more expeditiously. Every month of delay adds approximately $125 per unit in carrying and opportunity costs. *Using the builders'/developers' responses to establish an outside range for the costs of delay, we estimate the costs to be up to $1,125 per unit for subdivision waivers and variances; $1,188 for zoning-change applications; and $150 per unit for environmental reviews. That is a total of almost $2,500 per unit.*

The sum of all the excessive costs itemized above is roughly $19,500 per unit, on average, in New Jersey. That is higher than the $10,200 to $13,400 range estimated in the New Jersey case studies. *The difference between the survey and case study estimates provides a range for the excessive costs of regulation of between $10,000 and $20,000 per unit* (calibrated at the sample median new house price of approximately $236,000).

It is useful to place our estimates of the cost of regulation within the context of the literature. Of course, it is difficult to compare results from studies conducted in different places, at different times, and in different ways. Our study, for example, is unique in the broad way it defines regulatory burden and in its separation of excessive from normal costs.

Having said that, it is still reassuring that our estimates are of the same order of magnitude as other studies on the topic. We estimated plan preparation, application fees, and review costs to be approximately $19,000 per unit. Rosen and Katz (1981, 38) use $15,000 as their figure. We estimated that excessive time delays cost approximately $2,500 per unit. Johnston, Schwartz, and Hunt (1984) estimated delay costs to be $870 per month per unit, which corresponds to our estimates for a three-month delay. Finally, our gross regulatory cost (normal plus excessive) from zoning, subdivision, and environmental requirements is $38,375 per unit, or almost 16.3 percent of the median house price in our sample. The "unnecessary" or "excessive" elements of subdivision, zoning, and environmental regulation amount to $10,000 to $20,000 per unit, or 4.2 to 8.4 percent of the sample median new house price.

A 1995 survey of members by the National Association of Home Builders broke costs into seven categories that are not fully consistent with ours:

1. Land dedication/fees

2. Utility charges

3. Building fees

4. Development fees

5. Design standards and controls

6. Bonds/escrows/sureties

7. Impact analysis

The total per-unit cost of those items was estimated to be $12,289. See also *Joint Venture for Affordable Housing* (1985a, 1985d).

THE INCIDENCE OF REGULATORY COSTS

The preceding discussion does not address the short-run incidence of regulatory costs. The hedonic pricing literature assumes that all regulatory costs are passed on to consumers in the form of higher sales prices. In the long run, that seems to be true. However, our evidence suggests that developers seek to pay less for land where approvals are likely to be more costly. And, especially when regulatory costs are higher than expected at the time land was purchased (assuming land is purchased outright rather than with a contingency or secured with an option) and market conditions limit flexibility in the price charged for new housing, developers may be forced to accept a lower rate of return on their projects.

We explored the incidence question in several ways. We asked builders/developers how they factor prior approvals and improvements into their offer price for different types of land. The gap between approved lots and unapproved lots ranged from approximately $2,000 per half-acre lot when a $125,000 home was planned to approximately $39,000 per two-acre lot when a $750,000 home was planned.

The case studies drove home the importance of "bottom fishing" and "bargain hunting" for land. The New Jersey developers who weathered the recession of the late 1980s and early 1990s and are profitable in the face of a regulatory burden are politically savvy and well connected locally. In addition, they have sufficient capital to take advantage of opportunities such as discounted land owned by the real estate investment trust (REIT) or a bank, as well as other developers who need to liquidate land holdings. That is true in Chapel Hill, North Carolina, too. Successful developers in Chapel Hill believe that the restrictive environment works to their advantage, keeping competition out of the market.

We used the survey responses to construct rates of return on different types of projects. Higher-valued properties produce higher rates of profit, most likely because the price elasticity of demand for housing is relatively small for the highest-income households, allowing more of the regulatory costs to be passed forward to those buyers.

Another important consequence of a relatively inelastic demand for housing is that a dollar added to the price of land due to the capitalization of the required regulatory approval adds more than a dollar to the final selling price. That multiplier ranges from approximately two to six, depending on the value of the property being sold as well as on the way land price is measured (with or without improvements in place). In general, a multiplier of four is not unreasonable. When a developer expects regulation to cost a dollar (substantively or in procedural delay), on average he or she will attempt to increase the price of the house by $4.00.

The phrase "on average" is important, because our survey results showed a wide range of actual experiences among builders/developers. Of fifty-seven respondents to a question about the incidence of subdivision requirements, for example, nineteen indicated they changed the price they offered for land. Nineteen said they changed the pricing of units. Similarly, of sixty-four respondents, twenty-two said stringent zoning affects their offer price for land, whereas ten said it affected their selling prices. Seventy-four of 230 respondents indicated lower land price offers in response to environmental regulations, while thirty-nine said they charged more for a house. Moreover, the median response by all respondents was that environmental regulations reduced a developer's bottom line by 1 percentage point.

The general relationship between regulatory restrictiveness and market price was also demonstrated, albeit indirectly, in our regression results. More-restrictive communities issued fewer building permits, all else being equal. Presumably, fewer permits (i.e., starts) means higher prices for the housing that does get built or that turns over.

The key point is that the incidence of regulatory costs in the short and intermediate terms varies by project, depending on market conditions, the geography of supply, and other factors. In the long run, home buyers pay regulatory costs.

Our case studies provided other insights about who pays. Large, well-capitalized, experienced builders/developers maintain their bottom lines better than smaller firms. Indeed, when the housing market crashed in New Jersey in the late 1980s and early 1990s, many small builders were driven out of business, whereas larger firms were able to procure land cheaply and thus increase their market share and power. Those small New Jersey builders who have been successful produce in niche markets.

OTHER CONSEQUENCES OF REGULATION

One side effect of regulation was noted above: a shakeout on the supply side in New Jersey. In particular, delays that tied up their money made it difficult for small builders to stay afloat. Stagnant incomes at a time when housing costs were being pushed up also affected market demand. The end result was a spate of bankruptcies in the late 1980s. The fall in starts (see table 1) drove average prices up throughout New Jersey. The supply side in New Jersey is much different today than it was in the 1970s and early 1980s. An increasing share of the market is being provided by large builders/developers, such as K. Hovnanian and Toll Brothers. As we have demonstrated, it is those large builders who can affect the regulatory environment and prosper.

North Carolina did not experience such a shakeout during that time. The economy was buoyant, housing demand was more stable, and, with the exception of Chapel Hill, regulation was not as burdensome. Today, although large builders/developers are moving into North Carolina, many small mom-and-pop builders still operate.

Another consequence of the unevenness in the restrictiveness of regulation in New Jersey (as demonstrated in table 20 in chapter 5) is the variation in the rate of building among municipalities. The most restrictive communities have the fewest number of starts, often by design, and consequently, the highest prices. Towns that want to be exclusive bar new development, conveniently using regulatory apparatus as a means to exclude. That increasing exclusivity is demonstrated by our regression results: Exclusivity continues to characterize New Jersey despite the *Mount Laurel* litigation.

A third consequence of the high level of regulation in New Jersey is the changing mix of units brought to market. The slowdown in starts previously illustrated has been concentrated at the lower end of the residential price range. We explained the economics behind that: Higher-income households have lower price elasticities of demand, allowing builders to pass regulatory costs on to them more readily. To make a higher-priced unit attractive to the market, it must be enhanced. That was what some refer to as the "three-fer" phenomenon: Building a garage that can house three rather than two automobiles.

CONCLUSIONS

Our main concern has been with what we consider unnecessary or excessive regulation, not with regulation per se. We estimate the direct cost of excessive regulations to the developer to be approximately $10,000 to $20,000 per new housing unit, on average. The key question is how those costs are distributed in the short run among landowners in the form of lower land prices, developers in the form of lower profits, and home buyers in the form of higher housing prices.

There is no single answer to that question; local conditions dictate the impact regulations may have. If demand is robust and a developer is marketing houses for which there is a relatively low price elasticity, the costs are immediately shifted forward to buyers, with some multiplier. Using reasonable values for land's share in total housing production, as well as survey results, we estimated that multiplier to be in the vicinity of 4.0. That means that excessive regulation could add as much as $40,000 to $80,000 to the final price of a house.

If that were the case, there would be a direct link between regulation and the ability of New Jersey residents (especially first-time buyers) to purchase a home. In chapter 1, we gave the example of a home that would have sold for $175,000 but was offered for $185,000 instead, pricing 63,500 households out of the market. If that $175,000 home sold for $235,000 because of excessive regulation (adding the midpoint of the $40,000 to $80,000 range to $175,000), approximately 430,000 households would be priced out of the market, according to census income data. Those simulations are not far-fetched; they are consistent with homeownership trends in New Jersey.

Thus, if the impact of regulation is on households, there will be a fall in demand, especially at the lower end of the market. The supply side will respond by targeting the smaller number of higher-income buyers with units that provide greater margins, or by going out of business. Both of these phenomena have been observed.

We also have seen evidence that developers shift some or all of the $10,000 to $20,000 cost of excessive regulation back to landowners, who are often farmers at the urban fringe. Our interviews with developers and our reading of the land economics literature suggest that the shifting backward slows the rate at which land is converted to residential use. Therefore, once again a reduced supply of housing is being brought to market.

Finally, especially if developers have incorrectly forecast the regulatory costs they would incur, they may eat some or all of the excessive burden in lower profits. Indeed, all the developers we interviewed indicated they had lost money on some projects but were able to recoup that loss on another project. However, as we stated earlier, many developers have not been able to make up their losses and have gone out of business.

TOWARD AN AGENDA FOR POLICY ACTION

To reduce regulation that is unnecessary or excessive, we must first understand its causes. Our analysis, particularly in chapters 3 and 4, provides a basis for policy actions that could reduce some of the regulatory costs without reducing the benefits of regulation.

One issue that came up repeatedly was the discretion allowed local planning boards in establishing requirements. The Uniform Residential Site Improvement standards should limit some of this discretion and bring more predictability to the development process in New Jersey.

Most regulatory process problems can be corrected. In chapter 3, we identified three sources of delay: the competence of the participants; the capacity of the regulatory apparatus; and the institutional structure. (We ruled out complexity.)

Competence is judged for regulators as well as applicants. The better trained and more neutral local and state regulators are, the faster the review process can be. And the better informed applicants are about requirements and procedural steps to take, the less time they will lose.

Capacity refers to staffing levels. We observed serious bottlenecks in New Jersey, especially at the Department of Environmental Protection, due to inadequate staffing levels. Approval time and frustration levels would be reduced if review staffs were larger. The addition of trained staff could be an instance of money expended to save even greater amounts.

Institutional structure has several dimensions. One is the requirement for multiple layers of review (see table 8 in chapter 4). To the extent possible, multiple reviews should be eliminated. Towns and counties, as well as the state and regional regulatory organizations, should agree to consolidate the review of plans that fall in their common jurisdictions. The Memorandum of Agreement between the New Jersey Pinelands Commission and the Division of Coastal Resources of the Department of Environmental Protection, finalized in February 1988, is a good example. That memorandum consolidated review procedures for projects falling within the Pinelands area. Similarly, North Carolina's "one-stop" approach could serve as a model.

Another institutional arrangement that adds to the cost of regulation in New Jersey is the practice by local governments of charging developers for a municipality's review of plans and specifications. Not only is there no incentive to do reviews cheaply and efficiently, outside consultants may actually opt to spend more time than necessary doing them. The contrast between New Jersey and North Carolina in this area is marked: Builders in North Carolina spend several thousand dollars less per unit on those details.

One other institutional consideration is the role of public hearings and citizen input. New Jersey affords nearby residents more opportunities to appear before planning boards than does North Carolina. Not surprisingly, many more New Jersey regulators cited citizen opposition as a reason for delay than did regulators in North Carolina (see table 5 in chapter 4).

There are ways to streamline the hearings process without reducing citizen input. Public hearings do not have to be held each time there is a review of a plan element. Citizens should be brought into the process during the preliminary approval stage to ensure that any legitimate concerns are factored into the final plan. Another public hearing before final approval would be warranted to ensure that a developer has operated within the applicable ordinances and has addressed neighborhood concerns.

Several interviewees also addressed the affordable housing policies currently in place. There was a widely held belief that the *Mount Laurel* remedy is ineffective. Some housing has been built and rehabilitated and some zoning maps have been altered in response to the *Mount Laurel* litigation. (Of course, changes in zoning are *potentially* important.) But for the most part, New Jersey towns file their affordable housing plans with the state's Council on Affordable Housing, with no accountability for the actual production of those units. Even overlay zoning has not been an effective means to increase the number of affordable housing units in towns that do not welcome them.

The volume of affordable (*Mount Laurel*) housing built in New Jersey is related to the cost of conventional housing. Most of the units that have been built have been produced by developers as part of mixed-use projects, using cross subsidies, often in exchange for some concessions by the town. The higher the cost of conventional housing, the harder it becomes to make the economics work. Consequently, policies that succeed in eliminating the excessive cost of regulation will indirectly increase the volume of *Mount Laurel* housing.

Having made the foregoing recommendations, we must point out that, to a large degree, excessive regulation in New Jersey is a reflection of home rule governance. Communities that are not keen on new development have means at their disposal to slow the process down and otherwise make development more expensive, to the point of discouraging new projects. Developers can use the courts to prevent some actions by planning boards, but that itself is a time-consuming and expensive process. They usually simply decide to develop elsewhere.

We were struck in some of our case study interviews by the public's lack of knowledge about the real costs and benefits of new development. Several proposed projects for which there was vocal opposition would not have had the putative negative environmental consequences and would have generated fiscal surpluses for residents rather than the feared deficits. In addition, some of the *Mount Laurel* projects that were opposed would not have been occupied by low-income nonwhites but would have housed town service workers and elderly relatives.

Little can be done to sway people dead set against any new development, but public education programs can be useful in getting others to understand the real costs and benefits of residential development.

Appendix I

North Carolina Environmental Procedures

WASTEWATER DISPOSAL

Regulatory authority over on-site waste disposal systems is divided among state agencies and county health departments. Public and community sewage systems and systems designed to discharge effluent on land or surface waters must be permitted by the Department of Environmental Management under rules adopted by the state Environmental Management Commission (EMC). County boards of health permit and local inspectors oversee installation and final checks of septic systems under rules set by the state's health services commission. County board of health rules apply to all municipalities within their jurisdiction. For areas without central wastewater treatment facilities—a substantial percentage of the state—septic regulations may have a major impact on the extent and location of development.

FLOODPLAIN PROTECTION

Floodplain protection starts with a requirement for a locally granted permit for activities within a floodplain, with decision criteria specified by statute. Local governments are primarily responsible for establishing the extent of floodways and may request the assistance of federal and state agencies to perform the task. Where a floodway crosses municipal jurisdictional lines, the EMC may delineate the floodway. If the EMC determines that a floodway has not been properly defined by local governments, the EMC may, with thirty days' prior notice, set the bounds of the floodway, thus imposing the statutory restrictions. Municipalities are then responsible for enforcement of the statutory permitting requirements.

EROSION AND SEDIMENTATION CONTROL

North Carolina has retained control of erosion and sedimentation at the state level through a Sedimentation Control Commission (SCC) but also has concurrent local permitting. The statute confers rule-making authority on the SCC and requires that development erosion control plans be submitted to the SCC for approval. The law applies to any land use "that results in a change to the natural cover or topography and that may cause or contribute to sedimentation."[30]

While retaining direct state permitting authority, the SCC encourages and assists municipalities to adopt their own erosion control ordinances and to enter into interlocal agreements for that purpose. The statute directs the SCC to develop model local ordinances and approve only those municipal plans that meet or exceed the standards in the models. The SCC must approve local plans before they become effective, and local plans include the establishment of separate local agencies to administer and enforce local ordinances.

This overlapping jurisdiction over erosion control is coupled with provisions for direct intervention in implementation of erosion control plans if the SCC determines that the local government is failing to enforce a plan to its satisfaction. Even after an erosion control plan is approved by the SCC and a municipality, the SCC may compel a developer to make changes to the plan. After work has begun, if the SCC determines that an approved plan is not adequate to meet the requirements of the statute, it may require revisions.

WATERSHED PROTECTION

Watershed protection has become increasingly important in North Carolina as rapid population growth has increased the demand for potable water in developing areas. The policy statement of the watershed protection legislation states clearly that it envisions a "cooperative program of water supply watershed management to be administered by local governments consistent with minimum statewide management requirements established by the [Environmental Management] Commission."[31] As with other environmental affairs, standards are meant to be set by a state agency, with municipalities responsible for enforcement. Application of the watershed protection requirements is based upon those environmental considerations over local jurisdictional authority. One municipality may be required to impose restrictions on development within its territory to protect a watershed serving another jurisdiction. The state standards are meant to be incorporated into local ordinances. Permit-granting authority is local.[32]

Although cooperation is expected, the state has retained almost total control. The EMC writes the rules and model ordinances for watershed protection and has power to administer and enforce minimum state standards if a municipality does not adopt an adequate plan or does not enforce it to the satisfaction of the commission. The statute also provides civil penalties against municipalities that fail to adopt a required local watershed control program. The EMC may require that development permits granted by local governments be approved by the Department of Environment and Natural Resources (DENR) before they are issued.

ENVIRONMENTAL IMPACT STATEMENTS

In addition to any required federal environmental impact statement (EIS) mandates, North Carolina has imposed requirements of its own and has granted authority to municipalities to extend protection beyond either federal or state laws. The state requirements may apply in conjunction with those of the federal government, allowing one process to suffice, although separate EIS filings may also be required. Wetlands alterations, endangered species and habitat protection, navigable waterways, and other environmental considerations are affected by both state and federal rules, and permits from both levels may be necessary.

Local EIS impositions are intended to be supplementary and must exempt projects for which either a state or federal EIS is required. They may apply to any project undertaken by a private developer or "special-purpose unit of government,"[33] such as a public sewer or water authority. Local EIS ordinances may be incorporated into zoning or subdivision ordinances or may be separate. Local EIS ordinances must also establish applicability criteria; they cannot be required for any project not within those criteria.

The impact of local EIS requirements on residential development may greatly depend upon the local regulatory climate. The potential reach of municipal authority is very broad: Any project encompassing more than two acres may be subject to local EIS requirements. Meeting EIS mandates can be prohibitively expensive, requiring costly and time-consuming data gathering and analysis, as well as numerous public hearings and revisions to meet unanticipated and sometimes speculative concerns. However, there is no requirement for local EIS regulations, and administration is left to the local authorities, with no provision for state intervention. Thus, a local re-view can be as thorough or perfunctory as the local board desires. To date, only a few municipalities have chosen to impose local EIS requirements.

COASTAL AREA MANAGEMENT

The Coastal Area Management Act of 1974 (CAMA) established the basis for joint state and local planning for preservation, protection, and growth management of the state's coast. The Act applies to twenty eastern coun-ties, all abutting the Atlantic Ocean or one of the sounds.

Through the Coastal Resources Commission (CRC),[34] DENR adopted guidelines for planning within the coastal areas. Counties were respon-sible for enacting land-use plans consistent with those guidelines. If a county chose not to do so, CRC adopted one for it.[35] Local governments could also delegate responsibility to a regional planning agency. That organizational structure was supposed to give CRC effective control over how counties regulate land uses within the coastal zone. However, municipalities were not required to impose zoning and subdivision requirements consistent with plans approved by the CRC.

The CRC had a duty to designate "geographic areas of the coastal area as areas of environmental concern"[36] based upon statutorily defined environmental criteria. The designation places property under the restrictions of the Act. Any development within a designated area of environmental concern requires a permit under CAMA, in addition to any other permits that may be required. For minor developments—those of less than twenty acres for which no municipal sewer connection is required—a CAMA permit is obtained from the local permitting agency or from the secretary of Environment and Natural Resources if there is no local permitting agency approved by the CRC. All other development-ments[37] must receive a permit from the CRC, which may impose conditions on the permit.

All applications for permits must be submitted to the secretary, as well as to the local permitting agency for minor developments. The CRC sets submission requirements for all permit applications. Major developments require public notice and a hearing. The statute establishes deadlines that the CRC must honor when considering an application. Failure to act within the deadline results in automatic approval of the permit. The statute also defines the findings necessary for denial of permits, and failure to make the required findings again results in automatic approval of the permit. The applicant has the burden of proof at the hearing.

If an application is denied or approved with conditions unacceptable to the applicant, the law provides for an expedited appeal to court for a hearing on potential takings claims. On appeal, the CRC has the burden of proving that the denial or conditions were "not an unreasonable exercise of the police power . . ."[38] (White 1990).

Appendix II

Research Design

W e collected the data used in this book from a variety of sources in both New Jersey and North Carolina. Before we began the actual research, we spent a considerable amount of time developing survey instruments. We reviewed the questionnaires used in earlier studies (e.g., the National Association of Home Builders survey). We pretested several versions of the questionnaire in New Jersey and North Carolina, and we asked the Housing New Jersey Advisory Board for input and reactions. We also provided a toll-free phone number on each mail survey to encourage recipients to call the project staff with any questions.

We used a combination of qualitative and quantitative data that we collected through surveys and interviews with developers and builders, as well as local and state officials. In addition, we gathered data about New Jersey municipalities from secondary data sources to supplement the survey data. A detailed description of our data collection efforts is provided below.

NEW JERSEY DATA COLLECTION

Builder/Developer Questionnaires

We developed two types of survey instruments to gather information about the effect of specific types of regulations on the cost of bringing a housing project to market. The first instrument, which we called the short form, was meant to provide information about the effects of regulations on the typical project built by a respondent during the previous five years. The purpose of the survey was to get a general sense of the costs of regulations, as well as to measure the relative effect of zoning, subdivision, and environmental regulations on housing costs. Because we wanted information that would allow us to generalize about regulatory costs statewide, we drew a random sample from a frame of builders/developers registered with the New Jersey Department of Community Affairs. We mailed short forms to 200 of those individuals.

To ensure that our sample was representative of the state as a whole, we stratified it by geographic region. We employed an interval sampling strategy to create a random sample of builders/developers within each of four regions: the New York commuting shed; the Route 1 corridor; the Philadelphia commuting shed; and all other parts of the state. Fifty-eight (29.0 percent) of the 200 short forms were returned. However, not every form was completely filled in, so the number of usable responses for any one question was well below fifty-eight.

We developed a second, longer questionnaire to ask respondents specific questions about the effect of regulations on a project they had brought to market in the previous year. In addition, the respondents were asked who ultimately paid for any additional costs associated with the regulations. Since the answers to the long form were to be used to assess the effect of varying levels of local regulations on housing costs across New Jersey municipalities, we needed a representative cross-sectional data set. We therefore used a methodology identical to that discussed above: an interval sampling strategy based on stratifying the frame into the same four geographic regions. That generated a list of 650 builders/developers.

As with the short forms, we had a relatively low response rate. Only seventy-seven (11.8 percent) of the long forms were returned, and many of those were not complete. Thus, the number of usable responses to any one question was less than seventy-seven. We thought that the low response rate among long-form recipients was due to the amount of time it took to complete the survey. We conducted a second round of mailings using surveys that contained individual sections of the long form in an attempt to increase the number of usable responses about particular projects. We mailed 150 of these truncated long forms and had fifty-three (35.3 percent) returned. As with the other questionnaires, most of the returned forms were not completely filled out. Some respondents wrote that the form was complex and they did not have access to the kinds of detailed financial information needed to complete the questionnaire.

Planner/Engineer Questionnaires

We used questionnaires to gather information about the development approval process across New Jersey. We mailed questionnaires to a census of 150 local planners and engineers from a frame drawn from membership lists of a variety of professional organizations, such as the New Jersey chapter of the American Planning Association and the Association of Municipal Engineers.

Each questionnaire consisted of two distinct parts. The first section asked respondents about the time needed to approve project applications in their jurisdiction. The purpose of those questions was to gather information about the length of time it took regulators to process applications across a representative sample of New Jersey localities. We used the length of time to approve an application as a proxy for the overall level of regulatory complexity in any one municipality. Our initial intent was to see if development costs, as reported by builders/developers on the long form, were higher in localities that had longer approval processes.

The second portion of the questionnaire contained questions about the respondents' views of the regulatory process, designed to ascertain planners' and engineers' opinions about the amount of time needed to review project applications, the sources of any regulatory delays, and changes that might speed up the approval process. The answers helped us formulate recommendations for procedural and substantive regulatory reform.

Of the 150 questionnaires, only thirty-four (22.6 percent) were returned. Again, not every returned survey was completely filled in; we had fewer than thirty-four usable responses for any one question. Moreover, the low response rates for all of the questionnaires prevented us from conducting the analysis as we had originally proposed. We were not able to combine the information about specific projects with the results of the planner/engineer survey because of the low number of responses.

Secondary Data Collection

Due to the low response rate to our questionnaires, we conducted a second data collection/analysis effort in order to supplement the survey results. We gathered census information for all 567 New Jersey localities[39] and combined that data with information on school district performance drawn from the New Jersey Department of Education's School Report Card database. In addition, we combined census information with the New Jersey Treasurer's data on property tax rates and developable land at the municipal level. We also used data from the New Jersey Department of Commerce and Economic Development and information from the Department of Labor regarding single-family-home building permits issued at the municipal level. The data pulled from these sources was analyzed in a regression along with a variable that attempted to measure the regulatory restrictiveness of a municipality. That measure was constructed with the help of a telephone survey of local planners in which they were asked about the planning process within their jurisdictions. A random sample of seventy-seven New Jersey municipalities was drawn, and planners/engineers from those localities were asked questions about the regulatory process. The answers were used to construct a measure that categorized the localities as either restrictive or not.

Case Studies

Our data collection efforts included detailed case studies in order to gain a deeper understanding of how government regulations affect the development process in New Jersey. The localities studied—Princeton (Borough and Township), Mendham, Middletown, and Mount Laurel—were chosen with the assistance of the project's advisory board, which comprised individuals who had expertise about various aspects of the development process in New Jersey. The localities were not meant to be a representative sample of New Jersey but were chosen to illustrate the complexities of developing projects in areas that varied by the perceived level of restrictiveness.

In-depth, semistructured interviews with elected officials, planning/engineering staff, and developers were conducted in each locality in order to supplement the information gathered in surveys and secondary data analyses.

NORTH CAROLINA DATA COLLECTION

The research methodology used to gather information in North Carolina differed only slightly from that used in New Jersey. As in New Jersey, North Carolina data was collected through surveys and case studies. However, we did not use the long builder/developer form in North Carolina; neither did we collect secondary data on North Carolina localities.

Builder/Developer Questionnaires

We mailed 350 short-form builder/developer questionnaires to a sample of builders/developers drawn from a frame provided by the North Carolina Home Builders Association. To allow us to make comparisons, the instrument was identical to the short form used in New Jersey.

We oversampled builders/developers in the larger metropolitan areas of North Carolina (Raleigh–Durham, Greensboro–Winston Salem, and Charlotte) in order to gather data on builders/developers with experience in bringing projects to market in the parts of North Carolina that more closely approximated the New Jersey development process. We had a relatively low response rate from recipients of the questionnaire. Of 350 surveys mailed, forty-two (12.0 percent) were returned. As in the New Jersey surveys, many respondents did not supply answers to all questions, thereby reducing the number of usable responses to any one question. The low response rate was partly due to the fact that the sampling frame used did not include contact names. Follow-up phone calls helped to increase the response rate somewhat, but it was still low.

Planners and Engineers

We surveyed 125 North Carolina planners and engineers whose names we drew from membership lists of state professional associations. The survey instrument was identical to the one used in New Jersey to allow for comparisons. The response rate was relatively high: Sixty-five (52 percent) of the surveys were returned. However, many of the returned surveys were not completed. In addition, many of the regulations operative in New Jersey were not in effect in North Carolina. Nonetheless, the *lack* of regulations in many North Carolina localities was an interesting factor that helped to confirm our idea that the development process in North Carolina was quite different from that in New Jersey.

Case Studies

We conducted five detailed case studies in North Carolina in the same manner as in New Jersey. The five localities—Chapel Hill, Cary, Durham, Concord, and Jacksonville—were chosen to provide illustrations of the development process in different areas of the state as well as in localities that differed in their level of regulatory complexity. We conducted in-depth, semistructured interviews with elected officials, planning/engineering staff, and builders/developers in each locality in order to gain an understanding of specific issues faced by builders/developers in North Carolina.

Endnotes

1. We recognize, however, that enforcement of standard housing codes (BOCA or CABO, for example) can vary significantly. Burby and May (1996), for example, document different enforcement regimes among 819 local building departments.

2. 272 U.S. 365 (1926).

3. Indeed, the Kean Commission concluded that relaxing land-use restrictions would not generate new construction in cities because these restrictions are absent in cities anyway.

4. According to Briffault, home rule can have two legal meanings, both contained within a state's constitution. "The original form of home rule amendment treated the home rule municipality as an *imperium in imperio*, a state within a state, possessed of the full police power with respect to municipal affairs and also enjoying a correlative degree of immunity from state legislative interference" (Briffault 1990, 10). The second form "grants affected local government all the powers the legislature could grant, subject to the legislature's authority to restrict or deny localities a particular power or function. In a sense, it reverses Dillon's Rule—all powers are granted until retracted"(Briffault 1990, 10). Here, home rule is used more in the vernacular than legal sense.

5. North Carolina General Statutes (N.C.G.S.) §160A-4.

6. The New Jersey Municipal Land Use Law at C.40:455D-48 says "The plat and any other engineering documents to be submitted shall be required in tentative form for discussion purposes for preliminary approval."

7. During 1995 the New Jersey Municipal Land Use Law was amended by an Escrow Accountability Law with respect to plan review and site inspection services. The law gives a developer an independent appeal beyond the

157

municipality as to the proper use of the developer's funds and requires that the professional fees for review charged to the developer be reasonable.

8. Despite case law confirming this point, some municipalities still insist on installation of most improvements prior to granting final approval and prior to issuing building permits.

9. The figures are based upon U.S. Bureau of the Census, *U.S. Census Estimates* (Population Estimates Program, Population Division, January 2000). Those demographics give North Carolina the third largest rural population in the nation, behind Texas and Pennsylvania (Liner 1995, 22).

10. From the results of a telephone survey taken between January and May, 1994, reported in *Prospects for a Partnership for Quality Growth in North Carolina: A Survey of Existing County Planning and Implementation*, Paul David Stancil, 1996, p. 33. He obtained figures only for areas under the jurisdiction of county governments. However, incorporated cities and towns have the power to adopt zoning and subdivision ordinances. Thus, a city may have zoning within a county without any ordinance.

11. To prevent discrimination against one source of low-income housing, a municipal zoning ordinance may not prohibit manufactured housing, mobile homes, or trailers, but "may adopt and enforce appearance and dimensional criteria for manufactured homes. Such criteria shall be designed to protect property values, to preserve the character and integrity of the community. . . ." N.C.G.S. §160A-383.1 (cities); N.C.G.S. §153A-341.1 (counties).

12. Property may be placed in a conditional-use district only at the request of the owner. N.C.G.S. §160A-382 (cities); N.C.G.S. §153A-342 (counties).

13. N.C.G.S. §160A-381 (cities); N.C.G.S. §153A-340 (counties).

14. That could be a way for a municipality to permit a mixed-use, mixed-density project in an area previously zoned for single-family, large-lot development. The municipality and the developer could, by mutual agreement, establish overall parcel density and negotiate for public amenities, such as open space preservation. The municipality could protect its interests by imposing conditions on the approval, while the developer would not relinquish rights held under the existing zoning until all issues were settled. Another form of that type of zone is a PUD district, in which general performance standards are established for mixed-use development, with discretion given to the developer to design within the limitations of the district.

15. With substantial amounts of unincorporated area, cities and towns may annex new land, changing the reach of their authority. Annexation is allowed for areas that are not contiguous with the incorporated municipal limits, and across county lines. (That is known as a "satellite" annexation. N.C.G.S. §160-58.1 establishes the criteria the area must meet to be eligible for annexation. A city may choose to annex intervening sparsely developed areas, thus capturing areas of leapfrog sprawl.) No form of public approval, either from present residents of the annexing city or town or from those in the area to be annexed,

is required. The statutes establish technical criteria based upon the extent of development within the target area. If they are met, the decision as to whether to annex is up to the governing body of the incorporated city or town. Once annexed, a territory may become immediately subject to the incorporated municipality's land-use ordinances.

To protect landowners from the impact of possible changes in local land-use ordinances, North Carolina has specified statutory means for establishing vested rights, in addition to common-law vesting. The protections do not apply to the initial adoption of zoning or to its initial application to newly annexed territory. Issuance of a building permit for a structure will prevent changes in zoning from affecting that unit, as long as the permit remains valid. Approval of a site-specific or phased development plan will vest rights for a minimum of two years, and a city has the option of allowing vesting for up to five years.

16. CAFRA has some elements of a quasi-autonomous regional planning organization; however, it is under the direct control of the New Jersey Department of Environmental Protection, a state agency, instead of an independent commission.

17. Developers in New Jersey complained, for example, that they had to jump through two somewhat inconsistent hoops when developing in the Pinelands. That was verified in meetings with senior staff at the Pinelands Commission and DEP. However, both groups pointed out recent moves to devolve oversight for development in the Pinelands completely to the Commission, moving toward one stop approvals for wetlands permits and other approvals requiring state permission.

18. 67 N.J. 151, 336 A.2d 713, appeal dismissed and cert. denied 423 U.S. 808 (1975).

19. 92 N.J. 158, 456 A.2d 390 (1983).

20. Durham has chosen to impose such limitations in all relevant areas of environmental regulation. Such zeal does not necessarily lead to antidevelopment action, however. Development approvals in Durham usually take less than six months, and the city received consistently favorable comments from developers.

21. Table 4 raises the possibility that developers and regulators may be measuring the time for reaching a decision from different starting points. Developers may, justifiably, consider all the time from an initial request, while regulators may start the clock upon submission of a completed application.

22. We should point out that the North Carolina responses are "hypothetical" from the point of view of respondents, since multilevel reviews are rarely required in that state.

23. For example, our low response rates are about the same as those experienced by the National Association of Home Builders when it canvasses its membership.

24. The coefficient on the restrictiveness index is negative and significant (at a 93.3 percent confidence level). Since we scaled that variable to be dichotomous (low and high), with the low value meaning greater restrictiveness, the negative sign confirms that the more highly restrictive communities in New Jersey tend to have fewer building permits issued for new residential units, controlling for other factors that also influence building activity.

25. Detail from interviews with developers of low- and moderate-income housing is not included in this book but can be obtained from the authors.

26. The development company did in fact face an approval issue. Apparently, the previous builder had installed improvements without precisely following the plans approved by the planning board. When the developers we interviewed became involved, the town engineer insisted that corrections be made. They thought that was unreasonable since the engineer had inspected the work when it was done and had "as-built" drawings for more than three years. In addition, the work as constructed was fine, and the homeowners association did not want changes made to it. In the end, the developers did make the changes at a cost of about $40,000. We do not, however, consider that a cost of regulation.

27. They assume that a superintendent costs approximately $100,000 per year, including salary, benefits, insurance, and truck.

28. The builder believes that his friendships made it more difficult to get approvals on his project.

29. We admit, however, that there will be disagreement about what we consider discretionary or nonessential. Judgment is always necessary to operationalize a conceptual model.

30. N.C.G.S. §113A-52(6).

31. N.C.G.S. §143-214.5.

32. The EMC has created five categories for streams emptying into potential water supplies, ranging from WS-I for undeveloped drainage areas to WS-V for the upstream drainage basins of already-developed areas. Within WS-I, no development is permitted, and no sewer lines or wastewater discharges are allowed. For WS-V, the general restrictions applicable to streams and wetlands apply, with no requirement for other special protection. WS-II to WS-IV, covering increasingly developed watershed areas, are divided into two subcategories, general watershed and critical areas, with more restrictive rules for critical areas. For each of the subcategories, a municipality is given two regulatory options. One option, if stormwater controls are present, allows higher-density development, while the other option, without stormwater controls, limits the area to lower density. The choice of option is up to municipalities and may be implemented through zoning, subdivision, erosion control, or other police power ordinances.

33. Defined in N.C.G.S. §113A-9(2).

34. The Coastal Resources Commission is a fifteen-member body appointed by the governor. The qualifications required for each member are specified in N.C.G.S. §113A-104(b).

35. N.C.G.S. §113A-106 contemplates the adoption of the guidelines, while §113-107 establishes the criteria for the guidelines, with reference to the goals specified in §113A-102. N.C.G.S. §113A-108 requires consistency with the state guidelines and prohibits a county from issuing permits if they would be inconsistent. N.C.G.S. §113A-10: The timetable for county adoption of a plan allowed 480 days for completion. If the commission adopted a plan for a county, the county could subsequently enact a plan that, if approved by the commission, would supersede the Commission's plan. Counties could also opt to have their plans drafted by a regional planning agency and could delegate the responsibility for planning within incorporated municipalities to those local governments. A city that enforced zoning and subdivision ordinances within its territory could ask the Commission to compel its county to delegate plan-making authority to the city.

36. N.C.G.S. §113A-113.

37. These are defined in N.C.G.S. §113A-118(d).

38. N.C.G.S. §113A-123.

39. At the time of the survey, there were 567 local jurisdictions in New Jersey. In July 1997, Pahaquarry Township in Warren County was incorporated into Hardwick Township in Warren County, reducing the number of local jurisdictions by one to 566.

Bibliography

Apgar, W. 1990. The nation's housing: A review of past trends and future prospects for America's housing. In D. Dispasquale and L. Keyes, eds., *Building foundations: Housing and federal policy.* Philadelphia, PA: University of Pennsylvania Press.

Black, T., and J. Hoben. 1985. Land price inflation and affordable housing. *Urban Geography* 6: 27–47.

Briffault, Richard. 1990. The structure of local government law. Part 1. *Columbia Law Review* 90, 1 (January): 1 115.

Brueckner, J. 1990. Growth controls and land values in an open city. *Land Economics* 66: 237–48.

Burby, Ray, and Peter May. 1996. Regulatory styles and building code enforcement. Paper presented to APPAM Research Conference, Pittsburgh, Pennsylvania. November.

Deakin, E. 1989. Growth controls and growth management: A summary and review of empirical research. In D. Brower, D. Godschalk, and D. Porter, eds., *Understanding growth management.* Washington, DC: The Urban Land Institute.

Dowall, D., and J. Landis. 1982. Land-use controls and housing costs: An examination of Bay Area communities. *AREUEA Journal* 10: 67–91.

Downs, A. 1991. The Advisory Commission on Regulatory Barriers to Affordable Housing: Its behavior and accomplishments. *Housing Policy Debate* 2: 1095–1137.

163

Drummond, W., and M. Eliott. 1994. The effects of growth management programs on the prices of new and existing housing. Paper presented at the 36th Annual Conference Association of Collegiate Schools of Planning.

Eliott, M. 1981. The impact of growth control regulations on housing prices in California. *AREUEA Journal* 9: 115–33.

Farley, R., C. Steeh, T. Jackson, M. Krysan, and K. Reeves. 1993. Continued racial segregation in Detroit: "Chocolate city, vanilla suburbs" revisited. *Journal of Housing Research* 1: 1–38.

Fischel, W. 1990. *Do growth controls matter? A review of empirical evidence on the effectiveness and efficiency of local government land use regulation.* Washington, DC: Lincoln Institute of Land Policy.

Frieden, B. 1983. The exclusionary effects of growth control. *Annals of the AAPSS* 465: 123–35.

Fujita, M. 1989. *Urban economic theory.* Cambridge, UK: Cambridge University Press.

Goldberg, M., and P. Horwood. 1980. *Zoning: Its costs and relevance for the 1980s.* Vancouver, BC: The Fraser Institute.

Johnston, R. A., S. Schwartz, and W. Hunt. 1984. *The effect of local development regulations on the cost of producing single-family housing.* Environmental Quality Series, Number 31. Davis, CA: University of California.

Joint Venture for Affordable Housing. 1984a. *The Affordable Housing Demonstration: A case study—Everett, Washington.* Washington, DC: U.S. Department of Housing and Urban Development.

_____. 1984b. *The Affordable Housing Demonstration: A case study—Lacey, Washington.* Washington, DC: U.S. Department of Housing and Urban Development.

_____. 1984c. *The Affordable Housing Demonstration: A case study—Santa Fe, New Mexico.* Washington, DC: U.S. Department of Housing and Urban Development.

_____. 1984d. *The Affordable Housing Demonstration: A case study—Mesa County, Colorado.* Washington, DC: U.S. Department of Housing and Urban Development.

_____. 1984e. *The Affordable Housing Demonstration: A case study—Crittendon County.* Washington, DC: U.S. Department of Housing and Urban Development.

_____. 1984f. *The Affordable Housing Demonstration: A case study—Phoenix, Arizona.* Washington, DC: U.S. Department of Housing and Urban Development.

_____. 1984g. *The Affordable Housing Demonstration: A case study—Birmingham, Alabama; Knox County, Tennessee; Lincoln, Nebraska; and Sioux Falls, South Dakota.* Washington, DC: U.S. Department of Housing and Urban Development.

_____. 1985a. *The Affordable Housing Demonstration: A case study—Portland, Oregon.* Washington, DC: U.S. Department of Housing and Urban Development.

_____. 1985b. *The Affordable Housing Demonstration: A case study—Tulsa, Oklahoma.* Washington, DC: U.S. Department of Housing and Urban Development.

_____. 1985c. *The Affordable Housing Demonstration: A case study—Christian County, Kentucky.* Washington, DC: U.S. Department of Housing and Urban Development.

_____. 1985d. *The Affordable Housing Demonstration: A case study—Blaine, Minnesota; Boise, Idaho; Broward County (Coral Springs), Florida; Oklahoma City, Oklahoma.* Washington, DC: U.S. Department of Housing and Urban Development.

_____. 1986. *The Affordable Housing Demonstration: A case study—Fairbanks, Alaska, and White Marsh (Baltimore County), Maryland.* Washington, DC: U.S. Department of Housing and Urban Development.

Jud, G. 1980. The effects of zoning on single-family residential property values: Charlotte, North Carolina. *Land Economics* 56: 103–16.

Knapp, G., and A. Nelson. 1988. The effects of regional land use control in Oregon: A theoretical and empirical review. *The Review of Regional Studies* 18: 37–46.

Landis, J. 1986. Land regulation and the price of new housing: Lessons from three California cities. *Journal of the American Planning Association* 52: 9–21.

Levy, John M. 1994. *Contemporary urban planning.* 3d ed. Englewood Cliffs, NJ: Prentice Hall.

Lillydahl, J., and L. Singell. 1987. The effects of growth management on the housing market: A review of the theoretical and empirical evidence. *Journal of Urban Affairs* 9: 63–77.

Lindsey, Greg; Robert G. Paterson; and Michael I. Luger. 1995. Using contingent valuation in environmental planning. *Journal of the American Planning Association* 61, 2.

Liner, Charles D., ed. 1995. *State and local government relations in North Carolina.* 2d ed. Chapel Hill, NC: Institute of Government, University of North Carolina. p. 22.

Lowry, Ira S., and Bruce W. Ferguson. 1992. *Development regulation and housing affordability.* Washington, DC: Urban Land Institute.

Lubove, R. 1981. The roots of urban planning. In R. Lubove, ed., *The urban community: housing and planning in the Progressive Era.* Westport, CT: Greenwood Press.

Luger, Michael. 1987. State subsidies for industrial development: program mix and policy effectiveness. In John M. Quigley, ed., *Perspectives on local public finance and public policy.* Greenwich, CT: JAI Press, 29–61.

Maisel, Sherman, and Stephen Roulac. 1976. *Real estate investment and finance.* New York: McGraw-Hill.

Malpezzi, S. 1994. Housing prices, externalities, and regulation in U.S. metropolitan areas. Unpublished manuscript.

Mandelker, D. 1990. *Statement before Subcommittee on Policy Research and Insurance of the Committee on Banking, Finance and Urban Affairs. Hearing on regulatory impediments to the development and placement of affordable housing.* 101st Congress. Washington, D.C. August 2.

Mark, J., and M. Goldberg. 1983. *The impacts of zoning on housing values: A time series analysis.* Vancouver, BC: University of British Columbia.

_____. 1986. A study of the impacts of zoning on housing values over time. *Journal of Urban Economics* 17, 3: 257–73.

Miller, T. 1986. Must growth restrictions eliminate moderate-priced housing? *Journal of the American Planning Association* 52: 319–25.

Mills, Edwin. 1972. *Studies in the structure of the urban economy.* Baltimore, MD: Johns Hopkins University Press.

Mueller, D. 1989. *Public Choice II.* Cambridge, UK: Cambridge University Press.

National Association of Home Builders. 1995. *The truth about regulations and the cost of housing.* Washington, DC: National Association of Home Builders.

New Jersey Builders Association. Various years. *Dimensions.*

Nichols, J. 1981. Housing costs and prices under regional regulation. *AREUEA Journal* 9: 384–96.

Nichols, J., M. Olsen, J. Costomiris. and A. Levesque. 1982. *State regulation/ housing prices.* New Brunswick, NJ: Center for Urban Policy Research.

Pasha, H. 1996. Suburban minimum lot zoning and spatial equilibrium. *Journal of Urban Economics* 40, 1: 1–12.

Peiser, R. 1981. Land development regulation: A case study of Dallas and Houston, Texas. *AREUEA Journal* 9: 397–417.

Pogodzinski, J., and T. Sass. 1990. The economic theory of zoning: A critical review. *Land Economics* 66: 294–314.

Rosen, K., and L. Katz. 1981. Growth management and land use controls: The San Francisco Bay Area experience. *AREUEA Journal* 9: 321–44.

Rothenberg, Jerome; George C. Galster; Richard V. Butler; and John R. Pitkin. 1991. *The maze of urban housing markets: Theory, evidence, and policy.* Chicago, IL: University of Chicago Press.

Schwartz, S., P. Zorn, and D. Hanson. 1986. Research design issues and pitfalls in growth control studies. *Land Economics* 62: 223–33.

Seidel, S. 1978. *Housing costs and government regulations: Confronting the regulatory maze.* New Brunswick, NJ: Center for Urban Policy Research.

Star-Ledger. 1999. Excessive permit fees put homes out of reach: Jersey builders face layers of regulation. December 25, p. 1.

Somerville, C. T. 1996. The contribution of land and structure to builder profits and house prices. *Journal of Housing Research* 7: 127–41.

Stancil, Paul D. 1996. Prospects for a partnership for quality growth in North Carolina: A survey of existing county planning and implementation. Department of City and Regional Planning, University of North Carolina, Chapel Hill, NC. p. 33.

Stegman, M., with J. Brownstein and K. Temkin. 1995. Home ownership and family wealth in the United States. In R. Forrest and A. Murie, eds., *Housing and family wealth: Comparative international perspectives.* London, UK: Routledge.

Tiebout, Charles. 1956. A pure theory of local expenditures. *Journal of Political Economy* (October): 416–24.

U.S. Department of Commerce. Bureau of the Census. 1999. Housing vacancy and homeownership. *American Housing Survey.* Washington, DC: U.S. Government Printing Office.

U.S. Department of Housing and Urban Development. 1991. *Not in my back yard: Removing barriers to affordable housing.* Report of the Advisory Commission on Regulatory Barriers to Affordable Housing. Washington, DC: U.S. Department of Housing and Urban Development. July 8.

Wachter, S., and M. Cho. 1991. Interjurisdictional price effects of land use controls. *Washington University Journal of Urban and Contemporary Law* 40: 49–63.

White, S. 1990. *Affordable housing: Practice and reactive strategies.* Planning Advisory Service Report No. 441. Chicago, IL: American Planning Association.

Index

Page numbers in italics refer to tables.